First World War
and Army of Occupation
War Diary
France, Belgium and Germany

41 DIVISION
123 Infantry Brigade
Duke of Cambridge's Own (Middlesex Regiment)
23rd Battalion
3 May 1916 - 31 October 1917

WO95/2639/2

The Naval & Military Press Ltd
www.nmarchive.com
Published in association with The National Archives

Published by

The Naval & Military Press Ltd

Unit 10 Ridgewood Industrial Park,

Uckfield, East Sussex,

TN22 5QE England

Tel: +44 (0) 1825 749494

www.naval-military-press.com

www.nmarchive.com

This diary has been reprinted in facsimile from the original. Any imperfections are inevitably reproduced and the quality may fall short of modern type and cartographic standards.

© Crown Copyright
Images reproduced by permission of The National Archives, London, England, 2015.

Contents

Document type	Place/Title	Date From	Date To
Heading	WO95/2639/2		
Heading	41st Division 123rd Infy Bde 23rd Bn Middlesex Regt May 1916-Oct 1917		
War Diary	Southampton	03/05/1916	03/05/1916
War Diary	Le Havre	04/05/1916	05/05/1916
War Diary	Courte Croix	06/05/1916	29/05/1916
War Diary	Bailleul	30/05/1916	31/05/1916
Miscellaneous	23rd (Service) Battalion The Duke of Cambridge's Own Middlesex Rgt.	30/06/1916	30/06/1916
War Diary	Armentieres Sheet 36 C. 25a 7.9	01/06/1916	03/06/1916
War Diary	Le Touquet Trenches	04/06/1916	10/06/1916
War Diary	Armentieres	11/06/1916	15/06/1916
War Diary	Le Touquet Trenches	16/06/1916	24/06/1916
War Diary	Armentieres	25/06/1916	30/06/1916
Heading	23rd Battn. Middlesex Regt.	31/07/1916	31/07/1916
War Diary	Armentieres.	01/07/1916	03/07/1916
War Diary	Trenches 91-92-93	04/07/1916	04/07/1916
War Diary	Trenches 91, 92, 93, 96, 97, 98	05/07/1916	07/07/1916
War Diary	Trenches	08/07/1916	14/07/1916
War Diary	Le Bizet	15/07/1916	18/07/1916
War Diary	Billets Le Bizet	19/07/1916	23/07/1916
War Diary	Trenches 90-98 Le Touquet	24/07/1916	26/07/1916
War Diary	Trenches 91 to Gap C	27/07/1916	01/08/1916
War Diary	Billets Armentieres	02/08/1916	12/08/1916
War Diary	Trenches 91-Gap C	13/08/1916	17/08/1916
War Diary	Steenwerck	18/08/1916	18/08/1916
War Diary	Phinboon	19/08/1916	22/08/1916
War Diary	Gorenflos	23/08/1916	05/09/1916
War Diary	Gorenflos Meaulte	06/09/1916	06/09/1916
War Diary	Meaulte E. 12 a. Ref 62 D. N. W.	07/09/1916	08/09/1916
War Diary	F. 14 G. Sheet Albert	09/09/1916	10/09/1916
War Diary	Delville Wood	11/09/1916	12/09/1916
War Diary	Montauban	13/09/1916	14/09/1916
War Diary	In Action	15/09/1916	16/09/1916
War Diary	Montauban	27/09/1916	27/09/1916
War Diary	Flers	28/09/1916	29/09/1916
War Diary	Gueudecourt	30/09/1916	30/09/1916
War Diary	In Action	16/09/1916	17/09/1916
War Diary	E12. a. Ref. 62 D. N. W.	18/09/1916	26/09/1916
War Diary	Gueudecourt	01/10/1916	01/10/1916
War Diary	Montauban	02/10/1916	02/10/1916
War Diary	Mametz	03/10/1916	05/10/1916
War Diary	Mametz Wood	06/10/1916	07/10/1916
War Diary	Carlton Trench	08/10/1916	08/10/1916
War Diary	Eaucourt L'Abbaye	09/10/1916	11/10/1916
War Diary	Mametz Wood	12/10/1916	12/10/1916
War Diary	Dernancourt	13/10/1916	17/10/1916
War Diary	Merelessart	18/10/1916	19/10/1916
War Diary	Piebrouck	20/10/1916	21/10/1916
War Diary	Reninghelst	22/10/1916	22/10/1916

War Diary	St. Eloi	23/10/1916	29/10/1916
War Diary	Reninghelst	30/10/1916	02/11/1916
War Diary	Dickebush and Voormezeele	03/11/1916	08/11/1916
War Diary	Reninghelst	09/11/1916	15/11/1916
War Diary	Trenches 024-082 St Eloi	16/11/1916	17/11/1916
War Diary	Centre Battn Subsector St Eloi	17/11/1916	23/11/1916
War Diary	Chippewa Camp Reninghelst	24/11/1916	27/11/1916
War Diary	Dickebush	28/11/1916	30/11/1916
War Diary	Dickebusch and Voormezeele	01/12/1916	02/12/1916
War Diary	Reninghelst	03/12/1916	08/12/1916
War Diary	St. Eloi Centre Battn Sub Sector	09/12/1916	14/12/1916
War Diary	Reninghelst	15/12/1916	21/12/1916
War Diary	Dickebusch and Voormezeele	22/12/1916	28/12/1916
War Diary	Reninghelst	29/12/1916	31/12/1916
War Diary	Reninghelst Chippewa Camp	01/01/1917	02/01/1917
War Diary	Centre Battn H.Q. St Eloi	03/01/1917	04/01/1917
War Diary	Centre Battn Subsector St Eloi	05/01/1917	08/01/1917
War Diary	Reninghelst Chippewa Camp	09/01/1917	09/01/1917
War Diary	Chippewa Camp	10/01/1917	14/01/1917
War Diary	Dickebusch And Voormezeele	15/01/1917	21/01/1917
War Diary	Reninghelst Chippewa Camp	22/01/1917	27/01/1917
War Diary	Centre Battn St. Eloi Sector	28/01/1917	30/01/1917
War Diary	Centre Battalion St. Eloi.	30/01/1917	31/01/1917
War Diary	Centre Battalion Sub-Sector	01/02/1917	03/02/1917
War Diary	Chippewa Camp	04/02/1917	09/02/1917
War Diary	Reserve Battn Sub Sector	10/02/1917	15/02/1917
War Diary	Reserve Battalion Subsector	15/02/1917	21/02/1917
War Diary	Reserve Battalion Sector	21/02/1917	28/02/1917
War Diary	Chippewa Camp Reninghelst	01/03/1917	04/03/1917
War Diary	Centre Battn. Sub-Sector	05/03/1917	06/03/1917
War Diary	Centre Battn. Sub-Sector St. Eloi	07/03/1917	10/03/1917
War Diary	Chippewa Camp.	11/03/1917	16/03/1917
War Diary	Reserve Sector	17/03/1917	22/03/1917
War Diary	Chippewa Camp	23/03/1917	29/03/1917
War Diary	Centre Battn. Subsector	30/03/1917	31/03/1917
War Diary	Centre Battalion. Subsector	01/04/1917	05/04/1917
War Diary	Chippewa Camp.	06/04/1917	06/04/1917
War Diary	Godewaersvelde	07/04/1917	07/04/1917
War Diary	Arneke	08/04/1917	08/04/1917
War Diary	Bayenghem Les Eperlecques	09/04/1917	23/04/1917
War Diary	Arneke	24/04/1917	24/04/1917
War Diary	Godwaersvelde	25/04/1917	25/04/1917
War Diary	Chippewa Camp	26/04/1917	26/04/1917
War Diary	Reninghelst	27/04/1917	30/04/1917
Miscellaneous	Orders For Tomorrow's Operations By Lieut. Colonel. A. R. Haig-Brown. Commanding 23rd Battalion Middlesex Regiment.	15/04/1917	15/04/1917
Miscellaneous	Notes For Tomorrow's Operations by Lieut. Col. A. R. Haig Brown, Commanding 23rd Middlesex Regiment.	18/04/1917	18/04/1917
War Diary	Chippewa Camp Reninghelst	01/05/1917	01/05/1917
War Diary	Right Subsector St. Eloi	02/05/1917	11/05/1917
War Diary	H.Q. + 2 Coys: Dickebush Lake 1 Coy. Micmac. Camp. 1 Coy. GHQ Line	12/05/1917	14/05/1917
War Diary	As Over	15/05/1917	19/05/1917
War Diary	Alberta Camp Reninghelst	20/05/1917	25/05/1917
War Diary	Right Subsector St. Eloi	26/05/1917	30/05/1917

War Diary	Chippewa Camp. Reninghelst	31/05/1917	31/05/1917
War Diary	Chippewa Camp	01/06/1917	05/06/1917
War Diary	Left Sector	06/06/1917	06/06/1917
War Diary	Assembly Ground	07/06/1917	07/06/1917
War Diary	Advance	07/06/1917	07/06/1917
War Diary	Dammstrasse	07/06/1917	08/06/1917
War Diary	Blue Line	08/06/1917	11/06/1917
War Diary	Reserve Line	12/06/1917	20/06/1917
War Diary	New Fornt Line Left Of Canal	21/06/1917	24/06/1917
War Diary	Old French Trench	25/06/1917	27/06/1917
War Diary	New Front Line Left of Canal	28/06/1917	30/06/1917
Miscellaneous	Operation Orders By Lieut. Col. A. R. Haig Brown, Commanding 23rd Middlesex Regiment.		
Miscellaneous	41st Division A.	23/08/1917	23/08/1917
War Diary	Thieushouk.	01/07/1917	20/07/1917
War Diary	Westoutre	21/07/1917	14/08/1917
War Diary	Meteren	15/08/1917	20/08/1917
War Diary	St. Aples	20/08/1917	21/08/1917
War Diary	Setques	21/08/1917	30/09/1917
War Diary	Bray-Dunes	01/10/1917	04/10/1917
War Diary	St Iuesbald.	05/10/1917	05/10/1917
War Diary	Middlesex Camp R. 27. C3.3	06/10/1917	10/10/1917
War Diary	Oost Dunkerke Bains	11/10/1917	12/10/1917
War Diary	Newport Bains.	12/10/1917	15/10/1917
War Diary	La Panne	16/10/1917	31/10/1917

W305/1294(2)

41ST DIVISION
123RD INFY BDE

23RD BN MIDDLESEX REGT

MAY 1916 - ~~DEC 1918~~ OCT 1917
MAR 1918   1919 FEB

IN ITALY 1917 NOV — 1918 FEB

TO 122 BDE 41 DIV

2639

Original

23rd Bn The Middlesex Reg't

23 RFF
XLI Vol 1

Army Form C.2118

WAR DIARY
or
INTELLIGENCE SUMMARY
12/3/41

(Erase heading not required.)

Instructions regarding War Diaries and Intelligence Summaries are contained in F.S. Regs., Part II. and the Staff Manual respectively. Title Pages will be prepared in manuscript.

Place	Date	Hour	Summary of Events and Information	Remarks and references to Appendices
Southampton	3.5.16	4.30 pm	Embarked for France. Lieut Col G.C. Ash. D.S.O. Major Haig-Brown Lieut H. Farncombe R.A.M.C. Adjutant Capt H.W.B. Warneford Quartermaster Lieut R.W.T. Osmond A. Company B Company "C" Company "D" Company Capt W. Hoad Capt. A.V.A. Gayer Major E. Knapp Capt. A.A. Clarke Lieut D.V. Johnson " G.S. Lardner Capt. M.N. Lello 2nd Lieut A.C. Vaughan 2nd Lieut T.W. Purvis 2nd Lieut G.B. Smith Lieut C.W. Hardman 2nd Lieut F.N. Inwood 2nd Lieut C.F.G. Billbrough 2nd Lieut M.P. Ayatt Lieut T.H. Cooper 2nd Lieut L.R. Nixon 2nd Lieut D.J. Hamilton 2nd Lieut H.V. Bent 2nd Lieut E.T. Grear 2nd Lieut E.D. Perodeau 2nd Lieut F. Morris 2nd Lieut H. Bingle Attached Attached Attached Attached Lieut F.W. Brown 2nd Lieut W.H. Moran 2nd Lieut H.T. Snell Lieut K.G. Livingstone " J.W. Waterer Officers - - - 32 Other Ranks - - 949	

Army Form C. 2118

WAR DIARY
or
INTELLIGENCE SUMMARY
(Erase heading not required.)

Place	Date	Hour	Summary of Events and Information	Remarks and references to Appendices
Le HAVRE	4.5.16	12.15pm	Marched to Rest Camp No 5.	
Le HAVRE	5.5.16	4.a.m.	Paraded for entrainment	
COURTE CROIX FLETRE	6.5.16	9.30am	Billets	
"	7.5.16		"	
"	8.5.16		" a draft of 15 men arrived and were posted to C. Coys.	
"	9.5.16		"	
"	10.5.16		"	
"	11.5.16		"	
"	12.5.16		"	
"	13.5.16		"	
"	14.5.16		" C.O., Adjt., & M.O. in trenches at LE TOUQUET	
"	15.5.16		"	
"	16.5.16		" C.O. Adjt. & M.O. returned to billets	
"	17.5.16	7.45 pm	" The following message received — Gas reported to New Zealand Division, Not yet confirmed	
"	18.5.16	6.55pm	" The following message received — There is a probability that the Brigade may receive orders to move at short notice to reinforce another part of the line	

Army Form C. 2118

WAR DIARY
or
INTELLIGENCE SUMMARY
(Erase heading not required.)

Place	Date	Hour	Summary of Events and Information	Remarks and references to Appendices
COURTE CROIX	19/5/16	—	BILLETS Inspection at 11.15 am. by G.O.C. II Corps. (Sir Charles Ferguson)	
"	20/5/16	—	"	
"	21/5/16	—	"	
"	22/5/16	—	"	
"	23/5/16	—	"	
"	24/5/16	—	C.O. 2 i.c. Command Company Commanders in Trenches at LE TOUQUET	
"	25/5/16	—		
"	26/5/16	—		
"	27/5/16	—		
"	28/5/16	—		
"	29/5/16	4.30 pm	Battn paraded to march to billets in BAILLEUL	
BAILLEUL	30/5/16	—	Billets	
"	31/5/16	3.30 pm	Battn paraded to march to billets in ARMENTIERES and LE BIZET to relieve 1 S.A. I	

23rd(Service) Battalion The Duke of Cambridge's Own Middlesex Rgt.

To:-

   D.A.A.G.
      3rd Echelon, BASE.

Vol 2

          Herewith WAR DIARY of 23rd Middlesex Regiment for the Month of June 1916.

In the Field.   [signature]   Lt. Col.
30/6/16.   23rd Middlesex Regiment.

WAR DIARY or INTELLIGENCE SUMMARY

Army Form C. 2118

Instructions regarding War Diaries and Intelligence Summaries are contained in F.S. Regs., Part II. and the Staff Manual respectively. Title Pages will be prepared in manuscript.

(Erase heading not required.)

Place	Date	Hour	Summary of Events and Information	Remarks and references to Appendices
ARMENTIERES Sheet 36 C 25 a 7.9	1-6-16		Billets	
- do -	2-6-16		"	
- do -	3-6-16		"	
LE TOUQUET TRENCHES	4-6-15	12.25 am	Took over LE TOUQUET Trenches from 20th No. D.L.I. The N.Z. Brigade South of R.L.Y's on our Right. The 11th B'n The Queen's Reg'n on our Left	
"	5-6-16			
"	6-6-16		Casualties 1 O.R. Wounded	
"	7-6-16		Casualties Wounded O.R. 3	
"	8-6-16			
"	9-6-16		Casualties Wounded O.R. 2	
"	10-6-16	10 pm	Relieved by the 20" D.L.I. From 1.30 - 4 pm Enemy shelled LE TOUQUET station with 5.9 at the rate about 4 a minute. D. Coy in the cellars at the time. No casualties. The O.P. shed was destroyed Casualties Wounded O.R. 4	
ARMENTIERES	11-6-16		Billets Wounded O.R. 1	
"	12-6-16		"	
"	13-6-16		"	
"	14-6-16		" Wounded O.R. 1. Time was advanced one hour at 11 pm	
"	15-6-16		"	
LE TOUQUET TRENCHES	16-6-16	11.45 pm	Our artillery shelled the enemy's trenches at [?] #9 UP LINES on our right for about ½ hour when a successful raid was carried out by the N.Z. Brigade	
	17-6-16	12.10 am 5.15 am	A gas alarm was sounded No 1 on trenches and taken up down the line. No gas came over No A gas alarm sounded and No gas came over.	

W.C.A. [?] Lt. Col. 23rd Middlesex Regt. 3/6/16

Army Form C. 2118

WAR DIARY
or
INTELLIGENCE SUMMARY
(Erase heading not required.)

Instructions regarding War Diaries and Intelligence Summaries are contained in F.S. Regs., Part II. and the Staff Manual respectively. Title Pages will be prepared in manuscript.

Place	Date	Hour	Summary of Events and Information	Remarks and references to Appendices
Le TOURET TRENCHES	17.6.16		The following officers joined the Battalion 2/Lt F.H. GANDER 2/Lt R.H. SHEPHERD 2/Lt H. WILSON 2/Lt E.W. HANBY 2/Lt C.T. BROWN 2/Lt M.C.M. FENTON	
	18.6.16		Casualties Killed O.R. 1 Wounded O.R. 1	
	19.6.16		Casualties Wounded O.R. 2. The following officer joined the battalion 2/Lt H.R. ODLING	
	20.6.16		Casualties OR Killed one	
	21.6.16		Casualties Wounded O.R. two Killed O.R. one	
	22.6.16			
	23.6.16		Casualties O.R. Killed one Wounded two	
	24.6.16	12 midnight	Relieved by 2.D.L.I. OR killed one wounded one Took over billets in ARMENTIERES	
ARMENTIERES	25.6.16			
	26.6.16			
	27.6.16			
	28.6.16		Casualties Wounded O.R. one	
	29.6.16			
	30.6.16			

23rd Battn. Middlesex Regt.

From:- O/C. 23rd Middx. Regt.
To:- D.A.G.   G.H.Q.   3rd Echelon.

Herewith War Diary for period - 1st. to 31st. July 19

In the Field
31st July 1916

........Lieut-Col.
Commanding 23rd Middx. Regt.

WAR DIARY 23rd (S) Bn Middlesex Regt.
or
INTELLIGENCE SUMMARY

Army Form C. 2118

Vol 3

Instructions regarding War Diaries and Intelligence Summaries are contained in F.S. Regs., Part II. and the Staff Manual respectively. Title Pages will be prepared in manuscript.

Place	Date	Hour	Summary of Events and Information	Remarks and references to Appendices
ARMENTIERES.	1-7-16		Billets	
"	2-7-16		"	
"	3-7-16		"	
Trenches 91-92-93	4-7-16	1.15am	Relieved 20th D.L.I. Relief was delayed on account of heavy shelling by the enemy, who evidently had information of the operation. ARMENTIERES was severely fired on in several places. The relief was completed without casualties. Casualties O.R. killed one, wounded one slightly at duty	
		12 noon	Battns on our left 11th Queens on our Right N.Z. Brigade	
Trenches 91,92,93 96,97,98	5-7-16	3am	Our line extended. Trenches 96, 97, 98 taken over from 11th Queens	
		12 noon	Casualties Nil	
"	6-7-16	12 noon	Casualties O.R. killed two, wounded two (both remaining at duty)	
"	7-7-16	11 am	General Lawford inspected our line	
		12 noon	Casualties O.R. wounded three evacuated sick 3.	

Army Form C. 2118

WAR DIARY
or
INTELLIGENCE SUMMARY
(Erase heading not required.)

Instructions regarding War Diaries and Intelligence Summaries are contained in F. S. Regs., Part II. and the Staff Manual respectively. Title Pages will be prepared in manuscript.

Place	Date	Hour	Summary of Events and Information	Remarks and references to Appendices
Trenches	8.7.16	12 noon	Casualties. O.R. killed two, wounded four.	
"	9.7.16		Casualties nil	
"	10.7.16	12 noon	Casualties. O.R. Wounded one	
"	11.7.16	12 noon	Casualties officers Lt Snell wounded, Lt Livingstone accidentally wounded. O.R. wounded two including one slightly at duty	
"	12.7.16	12 noon	Casualties O.R. wounded six including two slightly at duty and one accidental	
"	13.7.16	1.15am	Enemy heavily shelled our position with 4.2 Howitzers, Field guns and large trench Mortars, considerable damage to trenches on the night of our line and on 93.S.2. 7 Two Redoubt, SURREY FARM and LE TOUQUET STATION also shelled. On the Right the enemy sent out a strong Patrol and surprised the AILSA CRAIG Garrison. 1 N.C.O and 3 men were captured three men escaped, consequently the raid which were were to have made on the enemy's trenches the following night had to be put off	
		12 noon	Casualties officers wounded Capt. W HOAD. O.R. wounded eleven including six slightly at duty, prisoners four	

Army Form C. 2118

WAR DIARY
or
INTELLIGENCE SUMMARY
(Erase heading not required.)

Instructions regarding War Diaries and Intelligence Summaries are contained in F. S. Regs., Part II. and the Staff Manual respectively. Title Pages will be prepared in manuscript.

Place	Date	Hour	Summary of Events and Information	Remarks and references to Appendices
Trenches	13.7.16	8.30 p.m	A bogus message was sent from SURREY FARM to Gap C & 5 telephone, intended for the enemy to receive by his listening apparatus	
		10.30 p.m.	Dummy figures were shown on the parapet and heavy artillery fire was opened on the enemy's trenches. Enemy replied with artillery which heavy trench mortars doing very little damage. They were apparently been deceived or parted to take the bogus message	
"	14.7.16	12 Noon	Casualties O.R. Killed one, wounded eight, including three slightly at duty one O.R. evacuated sick	
LE BIZET	15.7.16	12.45 am 12 Noon	Relieved by the 2.O" D.L.I Casualties nil	
"	16.7.16	12 Noon	Casualties nil, one O.R evacuated sick	
"	17.7.16	12 Noon	Casualties nil, one O.R. evacuated sick	
"	18.7.16	12 Noon	Wounded O.R 2 including one slightly at duty	

Instructions regarding War Diaries and Intelligence Summaries are contained in F. S. Regs., Part II. and the Staff Manual respectively. Title Pages will be prepared in manuscript.

WAR DIARY
or
~~INTELLIGENCE SUMMARY~~
(Erase heading not required.)

Army Form C. 2118

Place	Date	Hour	Summary of Events and Information	Remarks and references to Appendices
Billets LE BIZET	19.7.16	12 noon	Casualties O R wounded one	
"	20.7.16	12 Noon 5 pm	Casualties O R one, shell shock 2nd Lieut FOSTER and 2Lt TROLLOPE reported their arrival	
"	21.7.16	12 Noon	Casualties nil	
"	22.7.16	12 Noon	Casualties nil	
"	23.7.16	12 Noon	Casualties Nil	
Trenches 90 – 98 LE TOUQUET	24.7.16	12 Noon	Relieved 20th D.L.I Casualties O.R. Killed one wounded two slightly at duty Battn on our ~~right~~ left 11th Bn The Queens on our right the N Z Brigade.	
"	25.7.16	12 Noon	Casualties O R Killed one wounded two including one slightly at duty – 2 Lieut Hanby struck off the strength (sent to England sick)	
	26.7.16	12 Noon 11 pm 12 Midnight	Casualties O R wounded one An enterprise was carried out from Gap C. by the 20th D.L.I ~~the party~~ consisted of 4 officers 155 O.R D.L.I and 1 officer + 90 O.R R.E artillery lifted and party left our trenches. the Enemy opened heavy artillery fire on our trenches and on No man's land owing to heavy casualties from this artillery fire the party returned to our trenches and the Enterprise failed. Very little rifle fire was opened by the enemy all the casualties were due to the shelling.	

1875 Wt. W593/826 1,000,000 4/15 J.B.C. & A. A.D.S.S./Forms/C. 2118.

Army Form C. 2118

WAR DIARY
or
INTELLIGENCE SUMMARY
(Erase heading not required.)

Place	Date	Hour	Summary of Events and Information	Remarks and references to Appendices
Trenches 91-76 S4PC	27/7/16	12 Noon	Casualties O.R. killed three wounded eleven including one accidental and one slightly at duty	
		10.40pm	Battalion took over the same trenches as before the internment of the line took place	
	28/7/16		O.R. killed two wounded nine including one slightly at duty	
	29/7/16		Casualties O.R. wounded one	
	30/7/16		Casualties O.R. wounded one accidentally	
	31/7/16		Casualties officers wounded. 2/Lieut. M.C.M. Fenton. O.R. nil	

W.A.
Lieut-Colonel
Commanding 23rd Battn. The Middlesex Regt.

Army Form C. 2118

VOL 1
23 Middlesex

WAR DIARY or INTELLIGENCE SUMMARY

(Erase heading not required.)

Place	Date	Hour	Summary of Events and Information	Remarks and references to Appendices
Trenches 91-G9C	1.8.16	12 Noon	Casualties O.R. Killed one	Received photographs from hart. of arrival of following officers on 8/7/16 and taken on the strength of the Battalion from that date. Capt E.H.A. SAMSON, 2nd Lieuts. P. CUNNINGHAM - A.F. BUNDY - A.S. FOSTER - A. DE TOWNSOND - A.D. TROLLOPE
		11.45pm	Relieved by 20th D.L.I.	
Billets ARMENTIERES	2.8.16			
	3.8.16			
	4.8.16		Evacuated Sick O.R. one -- Capt. J.H. HALLIDAY to ENGLAND Sick, One man under age sent to Base	
	5.8.16		Capt. E.H.A. SAMSON Struck off the Strength on Transfer to W. SOMERSET YEOMANRY	
	6.8.16			
	7.8.16		Sgt A.E. HOPKINS to ENGLAND for Commission	
	8.8.16			
	9.8.16		To Base under age one	
	10.8.16			
	11.8.16		A coy moved from Laundry LE BIZET to take over billets in factory C.19.d.3.5	
	12.8.16	10.50pm	The Battn relieved 20th D.L.I. 11th Queens on our left N.Z. Infantry Brigade on our Right	
Trenches 91-G9C	13.8.16	12 Noon	Casualties O.R. Killed two	
		9.45pm	B.0022 received (orders relating to relief of 125th Infantry Brigade)	

Army Form C. 2118

WAR DIARY
or
INTELLIGENCE SUMMARY
(Erase heading not required.)

Instructions regarding War Diaries and Intelligence Summaries are contained in F. S. Regs., Part II. and the Staff Manual respectively. Title Pages will be prepared in manuscript.

Place	Date	Hour	Summary of Events and Information	Remarks and references to Appendices
Trenches 91-59p c	14.8.16		O.R evacuated sick one	
	15.8.16	12 Noon	Casualties O.R. Killed one	
	16.8.16	12 Noon	Casualties O.R. killed one, wounded three including two slightly at duty. O.R evacuated sick one	
	17.8.16			
STEENWERCK	18.8.16	12.10am	Relief by 13th D.L.I. complete - Marched to Billets at STEENWERCK	
		3 pm	Paraded to march to PHINBOON	
PHINBOON	19.8.16		Route March and Company Training 2nd Lieut SHEPHERD to R.F.C. Struck off strength O.R. evacuated sick four.	
"	20.8.16		B.O.O. 23 received re-entrainment Company Training	
"	21.8.16		Company Training	
"	22.8.16		Company Training	
	23.8.16	2.30am	Marched from PHINBOON	
		2.30pm	Arrived LONGPRE, detrained here and marched to GORENFLOS (about 9 miles)	
GORENFLOS		7.45pm	Arrived at GORENFLOS	

Army Form C. 2118

WAR DIARY
or
INTELLIGENCE SUMMARY
(Erase heading not required.)

Instructions regarding War Diaries and Intelligence Summaries are contained in F.S. Regs., Part II. and the Staff Manual respectively. Title Pages will be prepared in manuscript.

Place	Date	Hour	Summary of Events and Information	Remarks and references to Appendices
GORENFLOS	24.8.16		Company Training. O.R. Evacuated sick from One	
"	25.8.16		"	
"	26.8.16		"	
"	27.8.16		"	
"	28.8.16		"	
"	29.8.16		"	
"	30.8.16	3.15pm	Inspection by G.O.C. 123 Inf Brigade. The Battalion attacking three lines of Enemy Trenches.	
"	31.8.16			

W.J.A.
Lieut-Colonel
Commanding 23rd Batt. The Middlesex Reg.

WAR DIARY or INTELLIGENCE SUMMARY

Army Form C. 2118

23 Middlesex

Place	Date	Hour	Summary of Events and Information	Remarks and references to Appendices
GORENFLOS	Sept 1st		Following Officers joined 2/Lts. J.G. Rodwell, S. Wales Smith, S.F. Rogers. Reinforcement Draft 66 OR.	
"	" 2nd		Reinforcement Draft 5 OR.	
"	" 3rd			
"	" 4th	4.30 p.m.	Inspection by G.O.C. 41st Division (3.30 – 5 p.m.)	
"	" 5th	10.20 a.m.	Transport moved off	
GORENFLOS MÉAULTE	" 6th	10.30 a.m.	Battn. marched to LONGPRÉ. Train left for MÉRICOURT 5.35 p.m. arrived 8 p.m. Reached bivouacs at MÉAULTE 11.45 p.m.	
MÉAULTE E.13.a. Ref. 62.D.N.W.	" 7th		Following officers joined the Battn. 2/Lts. J.B. McKinnon, A.S. Hutchinson, J.L. Sutherland. Reinforcement Draft 48 OR.	
"	" 8th		Capt. S.S. Jones returns to England, sick. 1 OR evacuated sick.	
F.14.d Méaulte ALBERT	" 9th	2.30 p.m.	Marched to camp at F.14.d. Arrived 4.30 p.m. bivouacs. 2/Lt. T. Ratcliffe left for England to join M.G. Corps.	
"	" 10th	9.45 p.m.	Left camp for trenches in front of DELVILLE WOOD. Relieved 10th Liverpool Scottish 2.45 a.m. Capt. W.H. Poole joined the Battn. 1 OR evacuated sick	
DELVILLE WOOD	" 11th	from 5.30 a.m.	Artillery forward constantly under shell fire. Casualties 2 OR killed 15 wounded. Reinforcement draft 26 OR	
"	" 12	11 p.m.	B.C. & D Coys left trenches for MONTAUBAN. Casualties killed 8, wounded 32 missing 9 OR. 4/C.W. Haddman left to join R.F.C.	
MONTAUBAN	" 13	3 a.m. 11 a.m.	2/Lt. E.D. Perodeau left trenches for England sick. A Coy left trenches for MONTAUBAN arriving midnight. 2/Lt. B.T. Foss joins Battn.	
"	" 14	11 a.m.	Battn. left MONTAUBAN via MILK LANE for CARLTON and SAVOY TRENCHES (assembly) 1 OR evacuated sick. 2/Lt. E.M.L. Sandeulett to R.F. Corps. 1 OR evacuated sick	

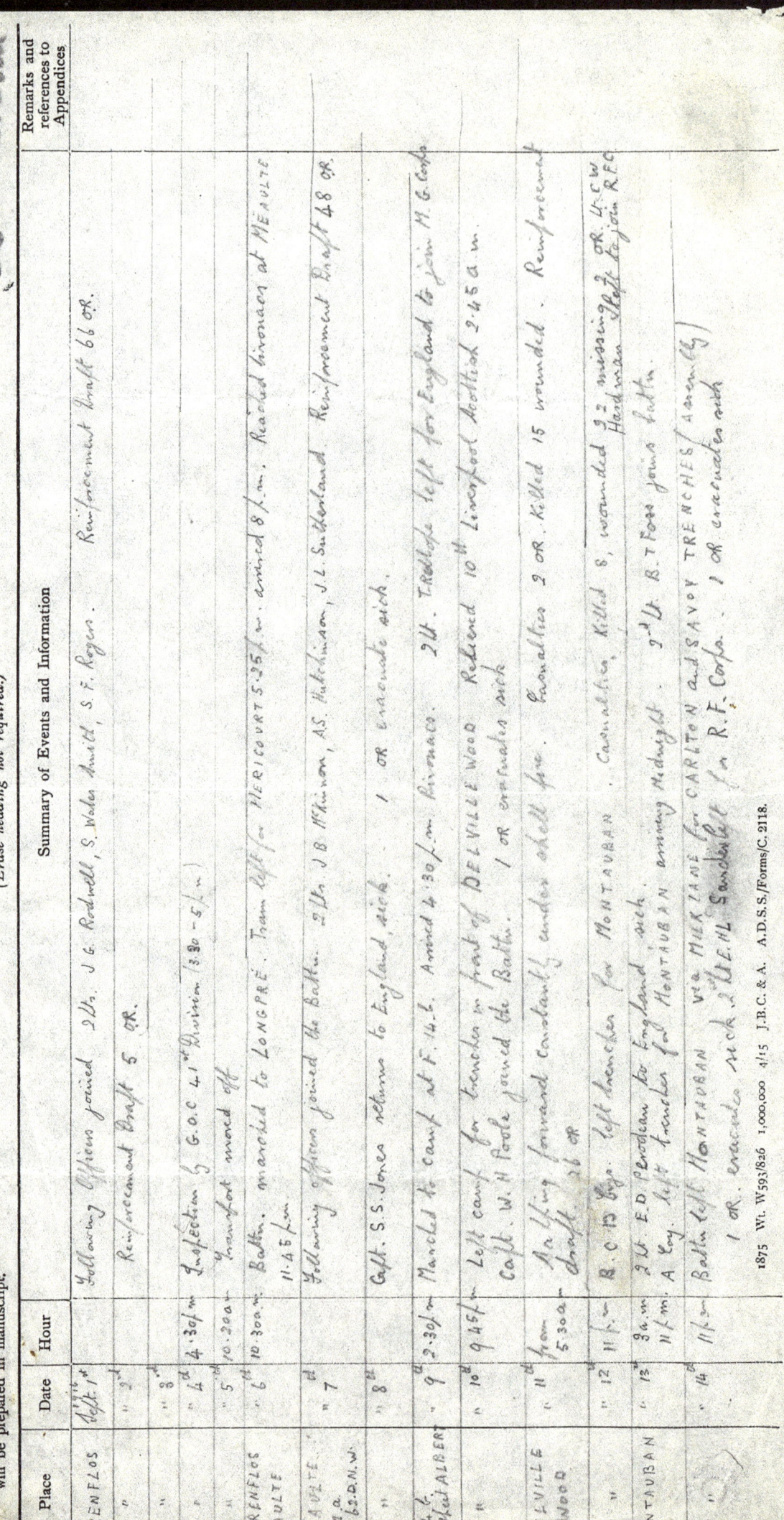

WAR DIARY
or
INTELLIGENCE SUMMARY

(Erase heading not required.)

Army Form C. 2118

Place	Date	Hour	Summary of Events and Information	Remarks and references to Appendices
In Action	15 Sept	1 a.m.	Assembly complete – 123rd Bde. in reserve of 41st Division and	
		6.20 a.	Zero – attack launched – 124 Bde on right – 122 Bde on left – tanks leading	
		10 a.m.	Bde. moved forward – to left of FLERS ROAD on line of our forward position in DEL- VILLE WOOD awaiting barrage. General Kenna	
		Midday	Left trenches for forward Switch TRENCH – heavy shelling. Adjt. casualty. B and D on right of FLERS ROAD, C and A on left	
			Enemy opened heavy shelling	
		3.15 p.m	Advanced up right of FLERS ROAD and along right of FLERS WOOD	
		4.30 "	B and D Coys leading with C.O. A and C Coys behind	
		5 p.m.	C.O. casualty. O.C. 'A' Coy ordered by Brig. General Clemson G.O.C. 124 Bde that the strong point N. of FLERS WOOD known as "Hog's Back" must be held at all cost. At N.E. corner of FLERS O.C. 'A' Coy met survivors of attack – about 950 men of various regiments – retiring.	
		5.30 p.m.	They were rallied and Hog's Back reoccupied with the left of B and D Coys.	
		6.45 p.m.	Ordered by Col. Oakley (O.C. 10 Queen's 124 Bde) to retire into line E. of FLERS at nightfall as the enemy was coming around the right flank.	
		7.30	Retired as to line stated. O.C. 'A' Coy (in command of Battn.) handed York 5 Lincolns over to Major Beatty (10th R.W. Kents). Held on during night.	
	16 Sept.		Heavy enfilade shell fire from dawn to midday and then at intervals.	
		6 p.m.	Relieved. Position to Bde. and asked for instructions and rations. Was ordered by Bde. to retire to SWITCH TRENCH at night	
			Casualties: Lt. Col. W.C.C. Ash wounded, Major E. Knott wounded, Capt and Adjt H.W.B. Wainford, Capt A.V. Gager, Lt. F.W. Brown wounded (Brown died of wounds 16/9/16), 2 Lt.	

Army Form C. 2118

WAR DIARY
or
INTELLIGENCE SUMMARY

(Erase heading not required.)

Place	Date	Hour	Summary of Events and Information	Remarks and references to Appendices
MONTAUBAN	27 Sept	7 a.m	Marched to bivouac between POMIERE REDOUBT and MONTAUBAN	
FLERS	28 "	Midnight	9 Lt. N.C.A Negrotti joined Batt. Relieved 6th Lincolns Bn. at FLERS AVENUE TRENCH.	
"	29 "		Reinforcement draft 5 O.R.	
GUEUDECOURT	30 "	4.30 p.m	Relieved the 10th R.W. Kents to the W. of GUEUDECOURT. 30 O.R.1 on left at N.19.d.9.7. 9th Leicesters on right at N.26.b.6.8. Held line each side of sunken road at N.26.a.3.8. to N.26.b.08. Enemy about 350 yds. distant.	Ref. British map from High Wood to GUINCHY

R. Naismith Major.
Commanding 23rd Middx Regt

Army Form C. 2118

WAR DIARY
or
INTELLIGENCE SUMMARY
(Erase heading not required.)

Instructions regarding War Diaries and Intelligence Summaries are contained in F.S. Regs., Part II. and the Staff Manual respectively. Title Pages will be prepared in manuscript.

Place	Date	Hour	Summary of Events and Information	Remarks and references to Appendices
In Action	16th Sept		H. Wilson and 2Lt N.P. Nixon Killed, 2Lts H.V. Bent, H.R. Odling, S. Wolverhampton S.J. Rogers, and Lt. H. Yarmcombe (R.A.M.C) wounded. O.R. 22 killed 129 wounded 32 Missing	
			Lt. J.T. Reader R.A.M.C Attached to Batt.	
	17th Sept	3.15 am	Retired to SWITCH TRENCH — which was occupied — occupied CARLTON TRENCH.	
		4.45 am	CARLTON TRENCH. Retreated to Bde. G.O.C. ordered me to fall back to GREEN DUMP and reorganise. Did so after leaving neglet reinforcement of 118 men sent up from transport line	
		10 am	GREEN DUMP and reorganised. Reported to Bde.	
E12.a, Rd. 62D.N.W.	18th Sept	5 am	Paraded (3 coders of Bde.) and marched to BECORDEL bivouac.	
		9.30 am	Arrived BECORDEL bivouac E.12.a. MEAULTES	
	19th "	3 p.m	Inspected by G.O.C. 41 Division	
	20th "			
	21st "			
	22nd "			
	23rd "	9 p.m	Reinforcement draft 6 OR.	
	24th "	3.30 p.m	Captain R.E. Oliver joins Batt.	
	26th "			
	26th "		Reinforcement draft 98 OR.	

Army Form C. 2118

WAR DIARY
or
INTELLIGENCE SUMMARY
(Erase heading not required.)

Instructions regarding War Diaries and Intelligence Summaries are contained in F.S. Regs., Part II. and the Staff Manual respectively. Title Pages will be prepared in manuscript.

Place	Date	Hour	Summary of Events and Information	Remarks and references to Appendices
EUEUDECOURT	OCTOBER 1st. 1916	3.15 p.m.	Zero. In conjuction with patrols of 20th D.L.I. and an attack by NEWZEALAND DIV. on our left, 2nd Lt. GREAR is sent out from our left Company with three patrols - 25 O.R. His orders are to ascertain if a small Salient in enemy forward line is occupied by day. If unoccupied, he is to seize the position; if occupied, he is to dig in 300 yards from Enemy Line. One patrol is to advance on the Right and one on the Left of the Salient- each distance some 850 yards. The Third patrol is to advance on the Centre of the position - some 300 yards. Enterprise meets with immediate and decided opposition. Enemy puts Barrage on our front line - knocking out 7 men with one shell - and opens vigorous M.G. Fire. 2nd Lt. E.J.L. GREAR is wounded when only 100 yards from our line. Left and Centre patrols suffer badly and control is lost. Right patrol, finally, actually succeeds in digging itself in 200 yards from enemy. Officer sent from Support Company to get information to what has taken place. On arrival at Left Coy. H.Q. he gets information that the patrols are disorganised and have suffered too heavily to continue the attack. A report with actual information from 2nd Lt.GREAR is sent to Battn. H.Q. Orders to withdraw. Searching parties sent out at dusk to collect remnants of patrols and bring in wounded. Relieved by 9th Fusiliers. Battn. returns to MONTAUBAN bivouac. Relief complete Casualties :- 18 O.R. Killed. 29 O.R. Wounded. 11 O.R. Missing. 2nd Lt. J.D. Hamilton and 2 O.R. evacuated sick.	N.20.a.7.3. Sheet 57cSW. $\frac{1}{20,000}$
MONTAUBAN	2nd.	10. am.	Battn. spends day resting, cleaning arms and equipment. The following Officer reinforcements reported 2nd Lts. G.BAINES, A.BEDINGHAM A.C.NEWMAN, W.ABBOTT, L.H. PORTER, H.L.BARCLAY, E.J.INGLEBY, C.C.IBBOTSON, F.GORE, A.M. KNIGHT.	S.20 Central.
MAMETZ	3rd	3 p.m.	Battn. marched to bivouac near MAMETZ WOOD.	
MAMETZ	4th		Major A.R. HAIG-BROWN assumes rank of Lt-Col. Reinforcement Draft 15 O.R.	
MAMETZ	5th		Recent Drafts instructed in precautions against Gas.	

Army Form C. 2118

WAR DIARY
or
INTELLIGENCE SUMMARY
(Erase heading not required.)

Instructions regarding War Diaries and Intelligence Summaries are contained in F.S. Regs., Part II. and the Staff Manual respectively. Title Pages will be prepared in manuscript.

Place	Date 1916.	Hour	Summary of Events and Information	Remarks and references to Appendices
MAMETZ WOOD.	OCTOBER. 6th		Training resumed. Work done on improvement of Bivouacs.	
	7th		Training and instruction of drafts continued.	
CARLTON TRENCH.	8th	10.pm.	Ordered to CARLTON TRENCH as Reserve. Arrive 11.30.a.m. Move forward to SWITCH TRENCH. A and B Coys. 30 yards in rear of SWITCH TRENCH; C and D Coys. in TEA SUPPORT. Officers sent during night to reconnoitre route to Front Line.	
EAUCOURT L'ABBAYE.	9th	4.30 pm.	Leading Coy. starts from SWITCH TRENCH to relieve 15th HANTS in front line N.E. of EAUCOURT L'ABBAYE. Relay system of guides breaks down soon after starting. Battn. stranded in TURK LANE until 10.30 pm. A Coy. alone meets a guide who taking wrong route, eventually leads them to the Trenches long before the rest of the Battn. A guide accidentally found. Relief proceeds. Enemy 35 to 200 yds. from our trenches. 20th D.L.I. on our Right; 47th Div. on our left. Casualties O.R. 2 Killed. 5 Wounded. Reinforcement Draft 34 O.R.	M.34.a.
EAUCOURT L'ABBAYE	10th	4.am.	Relief complete. Stokes Gunners warn us of their intention to engage Enemy Sap from which Snipers have been giving trouble. Companies stand to. Before a Stokes Shell has been fired Green Flares followed by Red are sent up by Enemy and hostile Artillery opens vigorous fire. Our Artillery replies. Stokes Gunners, after firing 2 shells, find it impossible to observe their fire owing to clouds of dust raised by Artillery. Artillery duel lasts half an hour. Consolidating position, joining strong points, wiring, done during night. Casualties :- Officers, 2nd Lt. A.M. Knight wounded. O.R. 4 Killed B.R. 9 Wounded.	

Army Form C. 2118

WAR DIARY
or
INTELLIGENCE SUMMARY
(Erase heading not required.)

Instructions regarding War Diaries and Intelligence
Summaries are contained in F. S. Regs., Part II.
and the Staff Manual respectively. Title Pages
will be prepared in manuscript.

Place	Date 1916.	Hour	Summary of Events and Information	Remarks and references to Appendices
EAUCOURT L'ABBAYE	OCTOBER 11th		Relief by 2nd BEDFORDS arranged at dusk. Relieving troops have difficulty in finding their way. B and C Coys are relieved and return to Camp at MAMETZ WOOD before dawn.	S.30 Central.
MAMETZ WOOD	12th	8.25.am.	Relief complete. The relief of A Coy. carried through in broad daylight in the face of severe sniping from the Enemy Front Line on account of their line being misdirected, A and D Companies return to Camp. Casualties :- Officers 2nd Lt. H. Porter wounded, O.R. 1 Killed 7 wounded 2 Missing. Are in reserve under orders to move at 1 Hours notice. Reinforcement Draft 26 O.R. 1 O.R. evacuated sick. Shelters and accomodation of Cam improved. Camp made ready to hand over to incoming Battn.	
DERNANCOURT	13th	11.am. 1.30.pm.	Battn. entrains for MEAULTE. Start march from MEAULTE to billets at DERNANCOURT. News of Lt-Col W.C. ASH'S death of Sept. 29th. 2nd Lt. D.C.M. CURTIS joins. Reinforcement Draft 64 O.R. Evacuated Sick 1 O.R.	
DERNANCOURT	14th		Brigadier holds conference of all officers in the Brigade. Schools for Specialist training formed. Special Sections formed for construction and drainage in the trenches. Pioneer Officer appointed. Capt. W.H. Poole transfers to 14th Northumberland Fusiliers.	
DERNANCOURT	15th		Specialist Training for trench warfare. Divisional General inspects Brigade and presents the following awards :- Military Medals. 1391 Sgt. Gould W.E. 932 Sgt Saberton G. 2771 Pte. Galley W.	
DERNANCOURT	16th	8.am.	Transport starts for MERELESSART. School continue training.	
Dernancourt	17th	2.30.pm. 5. pm.	Arrive at EDGE Hill to entrain for OISEMENT by 4.pm. Troops arrive and we proceed to entrain.	
MERELESSART	18th	11.30.am.	Detrain at OISEMENT, march to Billets at MERELESSART. Reinforcement Draft 10. O.R.	

Army Form C. 2118

WAR DIARY
or
INTELLIGENCE SUMMARY
(Erase heading not required.)

Instructions regarding War Diaries and Intelligence Summaries are contained in F. S. Regs., Part II. and the Staff Manual respectively. Title Pages will be prepared in manuscript.

Place	Date 1916	Hour	Summary of Events and Information	Remarks and references to Appendices
	OCTOBER.			
MERELESSART	19th	5.pm.	March to PONTRIMY and there entrain for GODEWAERSVEALDE at 7.30.pm. 1 O.R. evacuated sick.	
PIEBROUCK	20th	8.30.am	Detrain at GODEWAERSVEALDE and march to PIEBROUCK. Reinforcement Draft 23 O.R. Capt A.A. Clarke struck off strength on appointment as Adjutant to 15th Corps School.	
PIEBROUCK	21st		O.C. Companies and Specialist Officers inspect ST. ELOI trenches. General preparations for Trenches.	
RENINGHELST	22nd	9.am.	Battn. starts march to RENINGHELST and there take over hutments at ONTARIO CAMP. 2nd Lt. E.J.L. Sander rejoins after time of probation with R.F.C. 7 O.R. Evacuated Sick.	M.5.a.1.8.
ST. ELOI.	23rd		Relieved 51st AUSTRALIAN BATTN. in ST. ELOI LINE. 20th D.L.I. on right. 11th Queens on left. Composite Company of 3 Officers and 130 men of B and C in VOURMEZEELE AS reserve and garrison of that Village. Relief hampered by mud patch at O.29.	O.3.c.7.8. to O.2.c.6.8 Trenches O24 to O.33
		11p.m.	Relief complete.	
ST. ELOI	24th		Mud patch becomes worse. Two Stretcher Bearers to be continually on duty at Right of patch. System of Company Observers to replace day sentries adopted. 4 Observers post per Company to be chosen by O.C. Coy. Observers supervised by Sniping officer. Company Observers not to work at night.	
ST. ELOI	25th		Situation very quiet all day	
ST. ELOI	26th	5.am.	Inter Company relief. D Coy. from Support relieves B in front line. Relief held up by mud patch. Enemy opens fire with Rifle Grenades at B Coy. as thye wade through mud. Parapet at mud patch completely knocked in and	
		8.am	telephone wire broken thus left company isolated Relief complete. Casualties O.R. 2 Killed 8 wounded.	

Army Form C. 2118

WAR DIARY
or
INTELLIGENCE SUMMARY
(Erase heading not required.)

Instructions regarding War Diaries and Intelligence Summaries are contained in F.S. Regs., Part II. and the Staff Manual respectively. Title Pages will be prepared in manuscript.

Place	Date 1916	Hour	Summary of Events and Information	Remarks and references to Appendices
ST. ELOI.	OCTOBER. 26th		Advice received that His Majesty the King has been pleased to confer the Military Cross on No.12106 C.S.M. Bonothan and the D.C.M. on No. 348 Pte. Levy. In the former case for persistent good work in the face of the enemy; in the latter for conspicuous gallantry in leaving a front line trench unordered in order to go forward pass on a Lewis Gun the bearer of which had been put out of action and bring the bearer himself into the trench.	
ST. ELOI	27th		Inter Company Relief A Company from Support relieves C Company in front line. Relief complete 6.45.am. Orders for no one to cross mud patch by day. Route behind parados instituted for night. Casualties 1 wounded.	
ST. ELOI.	28th		Route behind parados of MUD PATCH improved by duck boards. Part of parapet built up. Casualties O.R. 1. Wounded. 1 slightly, at duty.	
ST. ELOI	29th	9.15	Telephone wire connecting left Coy. in front line mended. Relieved by 15th HANTS. B.C. and A Coys. relieved by day, D Coy. on left of front line by night. March back to ONTARIO CAMP. RENINGHELST. Relief Complete.	
RENINGHELST	30th		Battn. rests and cleans arms and equipment.	
RENINGHELST	31st.		Specialist Training recommences. Lt-Col. A.R. Haig Brown on leave to England. Capt. D.V. Johnson in command.	

W Johnson Capt.
Comdg 23rd Middlesex Regt.

23rd (S) Battn. The Middlesex Regt.

WAR DIARY for the Month of November 1916.
or
INTELLIGENCE SUMMARY

Army Form C. 2118

(Erase heading not required.)

Place	Date	Hour	Summary of Events and Information	Remarks and references to Appendices
RENINGHELST	NOVEMBER 1916. 1st	10 a.m.	Units of 123rd Brigade inspected by 2nd Army Commander. General inspects ranks, Battn. marches past in column of fours.	
		7 p.m.	G.O.C. 123rd Brigade holds conference of all officers. Details for training for trench warfare discussed. 2 Officers reconnoitre 2nd line defences of left sub sector. 5 OR transferred to 123rd M.G.C.	
"	2nd		Representative officers of Bgn. reconnoitre DICKEBUSH and VOORMEZEELE defences.	
DICKEBUSH and VOORMEZEELE	3rd		Battn. to be in reserve at DICKEBUSH and VOORMEZEELE. H.Q, B, and D relieve 3 Companies of 18th K.R.R. in billets in DICKEBUSH. A and C Coys relieve one company of the 18 K.R.R and 1 Company of 15th Hants in VOORMEZEELE. b/y the garrison of VOORMEZEELE to work only on the improvements of the dugouts and defences.	
		1.15 p.m.	Relief complete. Battn. to do special training to work at DICKEBUSH and members of schools to be exempt from fatigues. Training of a squad in rapid wiring commenced at VOORMEZEELE. 147ty R.E. working parties of 400 for night work. Reserve new that Little Hill E6 N.H. has won the military medal for great devotion to duty under heavy shell fire.	
"	4th	9 a.m.	More R.E. fatigues. Detail found impracticable owing to large number of men required by R.Es. As well as the daily salvo of "4.30" VOORMEZEELE receives a few "5.9s". 1 OR evacuated to base no under age.	
"	5th 4th	3.15 p.m.	Lewis Gun school alone able to carry on training. Registration of heavy trench mortars tasked by demonstration of field guns on RUINED FARM & considerable activity for an hour. Enemy reply with only a few shells. 1 OR wounded slightly at duty.	0.3 C 8.5

Army Form C. 2118

WAR DIARY
or
INTELLIGENCE SUMMARY
(Erase heading not required.)

Instructions regarding War Diaries and Intelligence Summaries are contained in F.S. Regs, Part II. and the Staff Manual respectively. Title Pages will be prepared in manuscript.

Place	Date	Hour	Summary of Events and Information	Remarks and references to Appendices
DICKEBUSH and VOORMEZEELE	NOVEMBER 6th	9 a.m.	Two officers and 70 O.R. start from DICKEBUSH to take over ECLUSE TRENCH from a small party of the 10th R.W. KENTS. Draft 3 O.R.	L 31, d, 8, 7 to look N° 8
"	7th		In the early hours of the morning our batteries engage enemy roads and communication trenches. In retaliation enemy open fire from RUINED FARM with 10 Round trench mortars on trenches O 24 to O 26 knocking down the parapet. Large fatigues for R.E's continue daily. Show for night work are unable to do anything on their arrival at their destination owing to trenches being filled with water.	
"	8th		A day's rain has filled most trenches with water. Some of the dugouts at VOORMEZEELE are flooded out. Cooker Battalion H.Q. flooded out of the BOLLAART BEEK. To add to the discomfort enemy fires 30 gas lachrymatory shells at the dug-out.	
RENINGHELST	9th	9.30 a.m. 1.45 p.m.	Relief by the 15th HANTS commences. Relief complete. Batt. marches to QUEBEC CAMP at RENINGHELST. Draft 6 O.R. 2nd Lt. BRTER rejoins.	
"	10th		Gas drill, training in rapid midens, cleaning of kit and equipment and inspection to check deficiencies of kit.	
"	11th	9.50 a.m.	B and C Coys. inspected by G.O.C. 123rd Brigade. "B" Coy. fouled in marching order. General orders parade to "B" and C Amos. take their caps off and put on gas helmets. He then inspected ranks, making each man who had not adjusted his helmet properly, fall out of the ranks.	
"	12th		Divisional general awards ribbons to 123rd Brigade. C.S.M. Baratham is awarded military cross for reorganising his company under very difficult circumstances at the battle of FLERS. L/Sgt HURS awarded military medal. Pte. LEVY, who is in hospital with wounds, has gained D.C.M. for very courageous bravery near GUEUDECOURT. Under	

1875 Wt. W593/826 1,000,000 4/15 J.B.C.&A. A.D.S.S./Forms/C. 2118.

WAR DIARY
or
INTELLIGENCE SUMMARY

(Erase heading not required.)

Army Form C. 2118

Instructions regarding War Diaries and Intelligence Summaries are contained in F. S. Regs., Part II. and the Staff Manual respectively. Title Pages will be prepared in manuscript.

Place	Date	Hour	Summary of Events and Information	Remarks and references to Appendices
RENINGHELST	November 12d		Very heavy machine gun fire as he left the trenches of his own accord and brought in wounded, restoring a L.G. from a wounded man to the rest of the team.	
"	13.		A small yellow balloon not capable of holding a man was apparently sent up from behind VOORMEZEELE. The wind took it slowly towards enemy lines. Three of our aeroplanes go up to investigate. One aeroplane circled round the balloon several times. It approached near enough to put the balloon out of action with machine gun fire. Having investigated, aeroplane returned to aerodrome. Balloon continued its flight until just over the enemy line; the hostile anti-aircraft guns open fire for first time on the balloon but did not appear to hit it. Balloon then slowly fell into enemy line.	
"	14d		Specialist schools continue their training. All Companies go to Baths. 1 O.R. evacuated sick.	
"	15d		Inter Company squad wiring competition. Brigade Commander present. 2/Lts NOBBS and A. ARTHURS join. V.L. ———	
TRENCHES 024-032 ST ELOI	16d	11.30	Relieved 18th K.R.Rif Centre battalion 2nd sector. Find that a new route over the top has been made to relieve trenches left of MUD PATCH. This route starts from OLD FRENCH TRENCH at the trench tramway. The latter part of the route is repaired in either side ——— with a wire to direct the leading man. Before relief is complete we supply 110 O.R. for R.E. working parties. Situation very quiet. Battn. stands immediately to commence strong points in the front line right of the MUD PATCH.	024-032 029-032
"	17d		Every available man not required by R.E.s is sent up to further to continue the work of building strong points. Ration parties cut down to a minimum, each party to make 2 or 3 journeys. Every man to work 8 hours a day. Every possible attempt is made to	

WAR DIARY or INTELLIGENCE SUMMARY

Army Form C. 2118

Place	Date	Hour	Summary of Events and Information	Remarks and references to Appendices
CENTRE BATTN. SUBSECTOR St. ELOI.	17th		Found the rest of the front line falling in. Wiring in right of front line. Officer patrol discovered working party near Craters 5 and reports to Lewis Gunners who disperse it.	
"	18th		Work on strong points continues at full pressure. 1 O.R. did sick.	
"	19th	1 a.m.	56 O.R. in trenches left of MUD PATCH relieved by similar number from the same Coy. They have made route overground very bad.	
		6:30am	Relief Complete.	
		9 a.m.	Twelve (12) men of our men attacked to 233rd Field Company R.E. arrive to help work on strong points. Casualties 1 O.R. wounded. 6 cases of trench feet from men just relieved from left of MUD PATCH. Lt. J.T. Reardon R.A.M.C. detached. Lt. L.J.S. Ryan attached.	
"	20th	1 a.m.	'C' Coy. in front line is relieved by 'A' Coy in support. Work on strong points on left of MUD PATCH impeded as at highest pressure. The carrying of material to this part of the line is difficult and takes a long time when the ground is wet. Draft 3 O.R.	
"	21st	2:15 a.m.	Zero. Artillery make a dummy raid. Concentrated fire for twenty minutes along craters and left of our line. On our front enemy artillery makes no response; his machine guns fire about 20 rounds. Draft 4 O.R. 1 O.R. killed	
"	22nd		Work on strong points continues with utmost speed. 2/Lt Barclay H.L. wounded. 11 O.R. evacuate sick. Orders received to relieve left of MUD PATCH 24th inst.	
"	23rd	10 a.m.	Enemy trench mortars our right front line and also shells it with 4.2's. Fairly generally enemy artillery activity greater throughout than usual. But by 11am for relief day	
		11am	Relief by 15th Hunts commenced	

WAR DIARY or INTELLIGENCE SUMMARY

Army Form C. 2118

Place	Date	Hour	Summary of Events and Information	Remarks and references to Appendices
CENTRE BATTN SUBSECTOR ST ELOI	23rd	11.30 p.m	Relief complete without loss	
CHIPPEWA CAMP RENINGHELST	24th		Men rest and clean their arms and equipment. Capt Clarke A.A. rejoins from XI Corps school	
"	25		Supply large working parties. No training possible.	
"	26		Leave increased. Baths allowed 13 allotments a week. 3 O.R. transferred to 128th M.G.C. Specialist training and close order drill.	
"	27th		Day spent bathing. Regimental Concert.	
DICKEBUSH	28th		Relieved the 18th K.R.R. in reserve. 2 Companies in VOORMEZEELE, remainder in ECLUSE TRENCH and DICKEBUSH. 15th Hants depart upon to be relieved by us in VIERSTRAAT SCOTT TRENCH.	
"	29th	10.30 a.m.	41st Divisional Artillery engage hostile trench mortars in front of right battalion sector. Operation lasts about half an hour. We continue to supply large working parties.	
"	30th		One more trench foot.	

Alan R Haig Brown
Lieut Col
O.C. 23rd Fusx

Army Form C. 2118

23 Middlesex

WAR DIARY or INTELLIGENCE SUMMARY
(Erase heading not required.)

Instructions regarding War Diaries and Intelligence Summaries are contained in F.S. Regs., Part II. and the Staff Manual respectively. Title Pages will be prepared in manuscript.

Place	Date	Hour	Summary of Events and Information	Remarks and references to Appendices
Dickebush Voormezeele	December 1st		Our batteries more active today. Many training for commission	
	2nd		Both enemy artillery and our own very quiet. The day has passed without incident. All men employed on R.E. working parties.	10R to England. 2 OR evacuated sick
Rent Haupiest	3rd		Battalion relieved by 15 Hants. Relief commenced 9.30; relief complete 1.15. Battalion returns to CHIPPEWA CAMP	
	4th		2nd CHIPPEWA CAMP much improved. Officers huts for Officers complete and are nearing completion. Officers can now be accommodated at the camp. A parade ground has been wired off and rolled	
	5th		Riding school for young officers recommences. Our working party day so no training in front line.	
	6th		Battalion allotted Baths. We are able to carry out drill and musketry training for the first time at CHIPPEWA having new parade ground. Men have a half holiday	
	7th		Most training found to be impossible owing to state of the ground. caused by rain in night. Saluting drill, some physical training, checking difference of R.E. 2 evacuated sick	
	8th		Baths allotted to battalion again. A half holiday granted	

31. W. Batt. Contest.
1375 Wt. W593/826 1,000,000 4/15 J.B.C. & A. A.D.S.S./Forms/C. 2118.

Army Form C. 2118

WAR DIARY
or
INTELLIGENCE SUMMARY
(Erase heading not required.)

Place	Date	Hour	Summary of Events and Information	Remarks and references to Appendices
ST. ELOI CENTRE BATTⁿ SUB SECTOR	DECEMBER 9th		Relieved 18 K.R.R. Relief of left of MUDPATCH complete much earlier than ever before. Relief complete 6 p.m.	
"	10th	3 p.m.	Considerable increase in enemy artillery fire on VOORMEZEELE sector. In retaliation to our fire on craters and artillery shooting on right of Brigade front, enemy shelled R line of right battalion keenly. Centre Battalion sector received only a few trench mortars and scattered shell fire including some 5.9's. The enemy is now using heavier shells than has been his custom lately in this district.	
		6 p.m. to 5 p.m.	41st Divisional Artillery carry out M.M.P. shoot. Bursts of field gun fire lasting a few minutes. 1 O.R. evacuated sick.	
	11th		Scattered enemy trench mortar fire on left our front line Companies. Early in the evening enemy trickles right front line Company's trench in 3 places. We put a stop to his hostility by firing rifles with the stokes. BLUFF SECTOR Rumbling heard but no enemy. A camouflet exploded by us in sector. Relief in front of trench O 28 discovered by enemy machine gun soon after. Working party in front of trench. 1 O.R. killed. Apparently enemy had noticed our men at stated work. He had taken out our previous night and placed a machine light concertina wire put out our previous night and placed a machine gun to cover that part of the mine. 3 O.R. evacuated sick.	

WAR DIARY or INTELLIGENCE SUMMARY

Army Form C. 2118

(Erase heading not required.)

Instructions regarding War Diaries and Intelligence Summaries are contained in F.S. Regs., Part II. and the Staff Manual respectively. Title Pages will be prepared in manuscript.

Place	Date	Hour	Summary of Events and Information	Remarks and references to Appendices
ST ELOI CENTRE BATTN. SUB SECTOR	DECEMBER 12th		Wet weather has made our right front line trenches of our left front Company even worse than those of our left front Company. Parties attached to R.E. from other battalions are sent to help the work of keeping these trenches from falling down. After dark right front line companies are overcrowded with numerous parties carrying, putting in A frames, revetting, and draining. 2 O.R. evacuated sick.	
"	13th		Unceasing work on right front line with good results. Normal activity on both sides.	
"	14th	9 o'clock	Enemy machine guns very active firing indirect on our ration track by CONVENT LANE. Artillery activity some little distance away on our right.	
		10.40	Orders from Brigade to stand to as enemy had occupied trenches O.71, 72, 73. Our own guns are now very active in retaliation.	
		11.25	Orders to stand down. Captain LELLO pronounced permanently unfit, struck off strength. 2 O.R. evacuated sick. 1 O.R. evacuated sick.	
RENINGHELST	15th		Battn. relieved by 15th HANTS REGT. Return to CHIPPEWA CAMP.	
	16th		Reinforcement draft 4 O.R. Company check deficiencies of kit. Half holiday granted.	
	17th		Training in musketry, drill, and specialist training.	

Army Form C. 2118

WAR DIARY
or
INTELLIGENCE SUMMARY
(Erase heading not required.)

Instructions regarding War Diaries and Intelligence Summaries are contained in F.S. Regs., Part II. and the Staff Manual respectively. Title Pages will be prepared in manuscript.

Place	Date	Hour	Summary of Events and Information	Remarks and references to Appendices
RENINGHELST	18th		Battalion transport inspected by Brigade Commander. 2 O.R. to England for Commission	
"	19th		Practice for inspection of Divisional General	
"	20th	9.15 a.m.	Divisional General inspects the Battalion at training. Numerous squads practising Bayonet fighting, Physical training, Drill, Wiring, Bombing, Lewis gun training and Musketry. Afternoon spent by Brigade practising for G.O.C. in C's inspection. Strength 300 O.R. for R.E. working parties. 7 O.R. evacuated sick.	
"	21st		123rd Brigade inspected by Sir Douglas Haig. The Commander in Chief seemed very satisfied with both the turn out and smartness on parade. 2 O.R. satisfied for Commissions.	
DICKEBUSCH and VOORMEZEELE	22nd		Relieved 18th K.R.R. in reserve. 2 O.R. evacuated sick. 1.15 p.m. relief complete.	
"	23rd		Enemy artillery activity has been greater than usual today and yesterday — particularly by his counter battery work. Much activity of our airmen. Nine aeroplanes seen in the air at one time. 1 O.R. evacuated sick.	
"	24th		Rev. Yames awarded Military Cross by Divisional General after having been previously recommended a few occasions. Enemy takes opportunity of bright moonlight of sending signal rounds for our batteries round DICKEBUSCH LAKE. 2 O.R. evacuated sick.	

Army Form C. 2118

WAR DIARY
or
INTELLIGENCE SUMMARY
(Erase heading not required.)

Instructions regarding War Diaries and Intelligence Summaries are contained in F.S. Regs., Part II. and the Staff Manual respectively. Title Pages will be prepared in manuscript.

Place	Date	Hour	Summary of Events and Information	Remarks and references to Appendices
DICKEBUSCH and VOORMEZEELE	DECEMBER 25th		The men Christmas Day is looked forward for the men until we are back in rest. In order to obtain a whole holiday, later work continues today as usual. Men however are provided with better dinners and the Y.M.C.A. at DICKEBUSCH supplies food very liberally to supplement other supply. Our artillery and stokes gun shoot carrier every to celebrate. 1 O.R. to hos under age. 2 O.R. to England for commissions.	
"	26th		Enemy puts a few shells into DICKEBUSCH trifidiving road wich over two DICKEBUSCH Company H.Qs are situated. 1 O.R. killed accidentally. 2 O.R. wounded.	
"	27th		Our guns in answer to the enemy increase their activity in a marked way. 26 O.R. sent to front line as wiring party also 13 O.R. to SHELLEY LANE Wiring of VOORMEZEELE SWITCH and MIDDLESEX LANE abandoned. Reinforcement 191 O.R. 1 O.R. to England for Commission.	
"	28th		Our guns again very active. Some enemy activity in the air.	
RENINGHELST.	29th	12.45	Relieved by 15th HANTS REGT. Relief complete. Battn. returns to CHIPPEWA CAMP.	
"	30th		Men's Christmas Day. 6 a side football tournament had to be put off on account of heavy rain. A concert after Christmas dinner followed by Brigade band the enemy.	

WAR DIARY
or
INTELLIGENCE SUMMARY

Place	Date	Hour	Summary of Events and Information	Remarks and references to Appendices
FENINGHURST	Dec 31		Working party day. Renewing officers go to Brigade School to see wire cutting demonstration with stokes guns.	

D Johnson Major
C 23rd Middlesex Regt.

Army Form C. 2118

WAR DIARY
or
INTELLIGENCE SUMMARY
(Erase heading not required.)

23. Middlesex

Vol 9

123/4

Instructions regarding War Diaries and Intelligence Summaries are contained in F.S. Regs., Part II. and the Staff Manual respectively. Title Pages will be prepared in manuscript.

Place	Date	Hour	Summary of Events and Information	Remarks and references to Appendices
RENINGHELST CHIPPEWA CAMP	JANUARY 1917 1st		Distribution of draft to Companies. CHIPPEWA BATHS allotted to Coys. Training in gas respirator drill and musketry. Obstacle course started. Battalion concert.	
		6 p.m.	Wire received that S.O.S. rocket has gone up on Left sector. Warning that Battn may have to stand to.	
		6.30 p.m.	Wire received resume normal conditions.	
"	2nd		Brigade Commander visited Companies while training and he desires that in future training should be, whenever possible, in the form of tactical schemes in the open, particularly regarding the handling of Lewis guns as covering fire in attack.	
		12.30 p.m.	Brigade Commander inspected draft and expressed himself very satisfied. Open warfare training during afternoon.	
DEWDREY BATTN H.Q. ST. ELOI	3rd		Relieved 18th K.R.R. in Centre Battalion Subsector Left Sector. Relief complete.	
		6.50 p.m. 6 p.m.	Owing to misunderstanding of code message from Brigade, it is thought that an enemy raid is expected and front line companies stand-to for 3 hours. A patrol then came in which made code message clear. Front line also reinforced by two Lewis Guns. 1 O.R. evacuated med.	
"	4th		Our guns very active in the afternoon on the left of Battalion sector. Very little enemy reply. Captain Oliver R.E. stands off strength	

Army Form C. 2118

WAR DIARY
or
INTELLIGENCE SUMMARY
(Erase heading not required.)

Instructions regarding War Diaries and Intelligence Summaries are contained in F.S. Regs, Part II. and the Staff Manual respectively. Title Pages will be prepared in manuscript.

Place	Date	Hour	Summary of Events and Information	Remarks and references to Appendices
CENTRE BATTN SUB-SECTOR ST. ELOI.	5th		Enemy guns active on the right of our sector. 2Lt FORSTER H.W. & FREEMAN G.C. join the Battn. Casualties 1 OR killed. 1 Reinforcement draft 10 OR.	
"	6th	7 a.m.	Enemy exploded camouflet in our sub-sector at O 2 d 1.8. Damaged part of our mine shaft. No damage to our trenches. Post listening post to watch shaft. 2.30 p.m. Medium Trench Mortars cut enemy wire on our right. 1 OR Evac sick	WYCHAETE 28 S.W. 2.
"	7th		Work on strong points and much mining continues. Sent working party to help 20th D.L.I. to mend damaged trench. 2 Lt PORTER took a Lewis gun and team on patrol with him and chased first row of enemy wire near RUINED FARM. Large enemy party dispersed at this point with Lewis gun.	
"	8th	9 a.m.	Enemy guns on VOORMEZEELE VILLAGE, the front of VOORMEZEELE SWITCH in our sub-sector and BOLLAARTBEEK dug-outs until 4.20. After half hour fire limited to VOORMEZEELE SWITCH and the dug-outs. Gunner of the SWITCH withdrawn to ECLUSE TRENCH without loss. 2Lt HUTCHINSON A.S. and 1 OR wounded in BOLLAART BEEK dug-outs shelling continued until 2.30 p.m. over 600 shells being fired. Dug-outs and shelters near BOLLAARTBEEK badly damaged. Comparatively little damage done to VOORMEZEELE SWITCH. Part of relief by 15th HANTS held up during the morning.	
		7.10 p.m.	Relief by 15th HANTS complete.	
RENINGHELST CHIPPEWA CAMP.	9th		Working Parties and cleaning of arms and equipment.	

WAR DIARY or INTELLIGENCE SUMMARY

Army Form C. 2118

(Erase heading not required.)

Place	Date	Hour	Summary of Events and Information	Remarks and references to Appendices
CHIPPEWA CAMP.	JANUARY 10th		Every man in 10 platoons fires Lewis Gun on range; every man in 6 Platoons thrown into tents. Two Companies practice tactical schemes in outposts and advance guards. 1 O.R. evacuated sick.	
"	11th		Battalion Concert. Remainder of Battn. (6 Platoons) fire Lewis Gun; six more platoons thrown into tents.	
"	12th		CHIPPEWA BATHS allotted to Battn. All Companies practice small open warfare schemes.	
"	13th		Anti-Gas Working Parties. Staff ride under C.O. Small open warfare problem studied. Lecture by Brigade Major to Kents and Middlesex Officers on open warfare and means of communication in an advance. 1 O.R. evacuated sick.	
"	14th		One Coy. is attached to 20 D.L.I. to increase their trench strength. With the 20th D.L.I. they relieve the 12th L. SURREYS in the night defensive subsector and are in support at SUNDERLAND FARM. Church parade.	
DICKEBUSCH and VOORMEZEELE	15th	9.30 a.m.	Relieved 18th K.R.R. in DICKEBUSCH and VOORMEZEELE. 1 Company and 1 Platoon in VOORMEZEELE; 2 Coys. and 3 Platoons in DICKEBUSCH. 1 O.R. wounded.	
"	16		Own artillery active all day on the left of the canal and more active than usual on our front. Enemy Parties as usual and using CONVENT and SHELLEY LANE. 1 O.R. wounded. Reinforcement Draft 70 O.R. 2 evacuated sick.	

WAR DIARY
or
INTELLIGENCE SUMMARY.
(Erase heading not required.)

Army Form C. 2118

Place	Date	Hour	Summary of Events and Information	Remarks and references to Appendices
DICKEBUSCH and VOORMEZEELE	17th		2nd day's bombardment of BLUFF followed owing to bad weather. Nevertheless our artillery occasionally active	
	18th	9.30am 7.30pm	Conference of Brigadiers and Commanding Officers at Centre Battalion Headquarters. Company attached to 20 D.L.I at SUNDERLAND FARM returns to DICKEBUSCH 1 O.R. evacuated sick	
	19th	11.20 pm	Our artillery became active damaging parts of enemy line along the whole Brigade front. Field guns had been pushed up close for this purpose. Two guns are stationed just behind S.P.3. from our front in reserve artillery preparation for 11 Queens anything party seems very thorough. German light signals seem very methodical and regular. Rockets bursting into one two or three green or red balls go up in turn along the enemy lines. 1 O.R. wounded	
	20th		All wiring parties concentrated on R. Line between BUS HOUSE and CRATER LANE 1 O.R. evacuated sick 1 O.R. wounded	

Army Form C. 2118.

WAR DIARY
or
INTELLIGENCE SUMMARY.
(Erase heading not required.)

Instructions regarding War Diaries and Intelligence Summaries are contained in F.S. Regs., Part II. and the Staff Manual respectively. Title pages will be prepared in manuscript.

Place	Date	Hour	Summary of Events and Information	Remarks and references to Appendices
DICKEBUSCH and YPRES/ZEER	21st		Supplementary S.O.S. signal to be single green asteroid rocket in future. Strong Point at trenches O.25, O.26, which had been practically completed by our fatigue attached to 233rd Field Coy R.E. is blown in by enemy heavy trench mortars. Reinforcement Draft 3 O.R. R.S.M. EASTER rejoins. 2 O.R. evacuated sick	
RENINGHELST	22nd		Relieved by 15th Hants. Battn. march back to CHIPPEWA CAMP.	
CHIPPEWA CAMP			10 O.R. evacuated sick	
"	23rd		CHIPPEWA Battn. and rifle range allotted to Battn. Owing to the hard frost the paths are unworkable and it is decided to keep the men warm by taking them out on route marches and tactical schemes instead of using the range.	
"	24th		Whole battalion on working parties	
"	25th		During the morning 100 O.R. march to 123rd Brigade school and are there instructed by the staff of the school in Drill, Bayonet fighting, firing supervision on the range, sniping and constructing loopholes and advanced fighting. In the afternoon another 100 O.R. are taught the same subjects. Lectures in the Brigade school Lecture Room by O.C. Companies on the Defence Scheme	

WAR DIARY
or
INTELLIGENCE SUMMARY

Army Form C. 2118.

Place	Date	Hour	Summary of Events and Information	Remarks and references to Appendices
RENINGHELST CHIPPEWA CAMP.	JANUARY 1917. 25th		Inspection of Brigade at training by Army Commander.	
"	26th		Battalion's day of rest. Too hard for football. Battalion Concert. Inspection of Brigade by Divisional General.	
"	27th		Whole Battalion on Working Parties. Officers reconnoitre OLD B. H. Q.	
CENTRE Battn.	28th		Relieved 18th K.R.R. Relief Complete.	
ST. ELOI SECTOR		6.40	Some hostile trench mortar fire.	
		3.p.m	Some hostile trench mortar fire & BENJAMIN on left of locality. 2 OR killed.	
		4.p.m	To men patrols go out in white suits. Raining	
"	29th		Three more trench mortars identified; one heavy and 2 medium. They are in a position to enfilade SHELLEY LANE and CONVENT LANE. 2 OR killed. 2 OR wounded (1 slightly at duty)	
"	30th		Heavy trench mortar has not yet fired since the Battn. has been in the line. Ground too hard to be able to do much work in the front line. Very difficult to secure in stakes so many carrots of thickening	

WAR DIARY
or
INTELLIGENCE SUMMARY.
(Erase heading not required.)

Army Form C. 2118.

Place	Date	Hour	Summary of Events and Information	Remarks and references to Appendices
CENTRE BATTALION Sr. ELOI	30		mine already put up. 2/Lt. NEGRETTI N.C.O.A. killed Altos. STONE and C.W. Thomas report for duty	
"	31st	12.35 a.m	Warning given to Companies to practice "Stand-to" Battle positions taken up and extra ammunition and bombs issued to the men. Company in reserve at VOORMEZEELE SWITCH took 35 minutes to take up their position in the R. Line and serve out bombs and S.A.A. Day passed quietly. During the afternoon the enemy energetically shelled SCOTTISH WOOD for counter battery purposes. Telephonic communication between companies and Battalion H.Q. is not allowed between until 3 p.m. Communication also forbidden between Battalion H.Q. and Brigade H.Q. Runners into relay	
		9 a.m.	posts and Winters are used to replace telephone.	

Chas R Craig Ronn
Lieut Col
O.C. 22 this [Regt]

23rd MIDDLESEX REGT

WAR DIARY for the Month of FEBRUARY 1917.

or

INTELLIGENCE SUMMARY.

Army Form C. 2118.

Vol 16

Place	Date	Hour	Summary of Events and Information	Remarks and references to Appendices
CENTRE BATTALION SUB SECTOR	1917 February 1st		Party of 25 O.R. from a company in reserve branch told off specially for salvage duties. Good results obtained. Water supply is still very difficult owing to hard frost. Arrangements have been made to thaw water in tanks at trench tramway. These are filled from watercarts running in the evening at VOORMEZEELE. Voorryst water also frozen in crest by the time it reaches VOORMEZEELE and has to be thawed. Hostile artillery still very active. Left on RIGHT and LEFT front companies, 2 O.R. killed & 8 wounded in right front company. 3 O.R. evacuated sick.	
"	2nd		Colonel returns from leave. An officer fatal stuns fire with a howitzer when a few yards from enemy M.G. Emplacement. Putting the enemy gunner out of action. During the afternoon artillery shoot on anything fed which has been causing so much trouble in No 3 CRATER. Observation and correction of fire by one of an officer from front line. Rupture pad successfully set, enemy rifles with a few mortars. 1 O.R. killed. 2 O.R. to England for commission. 2/Lt Smith G.B. gazetted Lieutenant with seniority from July 1st.	

Army Form C. 2118.

WAR DIARY
or
INTELLIGENCE SUMMARY.
(Erase heading not required.)

Place	Date	Hour	Summary of Events and Information	Remarks and references to Appendices
CENTRE BATTALION SUB SECTOR	1917 February 3rd		Relieved by 15th Hants Regt. Their first platoon arrived at 9.30 a.m. in DICKEBUSCH instead of usual time of 11.30 a.m. Relief with exception of LOCALITY, Coy Hdqrs 2 pl.m. No 2 arrived to relieve own platoon in the BUS HOUSE. Wire 12 E. Army's to do so (3.55 p.m.) Relief of BUS HOUSE not actually carried out until 6 p.m.	
CHIPPEWA CAMP	4th		Whole battalion employed as working parties. Church parade. Three/one enquiries.	
"	5th		4 OR Reinforcements. 2 OR evacuated sick. 2 OR to England on Commission. Coy now cleaning Kit and equipment after trenches, bathing at CHIPPEWA BATHS and checking deficiency of Kit. 5 OR wounded. 2 OR evacuated sick. 2/Lt. HINEY E.A. and BROOM F.J.H. join battalion.	
"	6th		Training in bombing at bombing pit. Extended order and attack practice by Companies.	
"	7th		Send 200 OR. to 123rd Brigade School for half a days training. Small squads in bombing, Lewis gun training, rapid fire on range, Anti-gas, Bayonet fighting and Physical training.	
"	8th		Hun aeroplanes have paid repeated visits to RENINGHELST and LA CLYTTE during the last day or two. Training in extended order and attack practice which the Batt. has now made possible. 2 OR evacuated sick. Coll. RINDLE to hospital	

WAR DIARY
or
INTELLIGENCE SUMMARY.

(Erase heading not required.)

Army Form C. 2118.

Instructions regarding War Diaries and Intelligence Summaries are contained in F.S. Regs., Part II and the Staff Manual respectively. Title pages will be prepared in manuscript.

Place	Date	Hour	Summary of Events and Information	Remarks and references to Appendices
	1917			
CHIPPEWA CAMP	FEBRUARY 9th		Whole battalion employed under R.E. on working parties. Officers and in working parties reconnoitre NEW G.H.Q. line.	
RESERVE BATT'N	10th		Relieved 18th K.R.R. in DICKEBUSCH and VOORMEZEELE. Usual hour of 9.30 pm 1 O.R. evacuated sick	
SUB SECTOR	11th	11.30 a.m.	Platoon to arrive at DICKEBUSCH changed to 11.30 a.m. Most of heavy shelling on the GRAND BOIS 2 O.R. evacuated sick.	
"	12th		Wiring parties work each night in front of OLD FRENCH TRENCH between CONVENT and SHELLEY LANES also road at O1a 25.10. 2 O.R. evacuated sick	
"	13th		Enemy entered centre battalion front line (about O.29) in day light and catches garrison at breakfast	
"	14th		Pioneers have been working night and day (in two shifts of 12) to construct 2 dugouts on bank of DICKEBUSCH LAKE at H.28.d.40.05 for Battalion H.Q. and dugouts when battalion states of public position from rest	
"	15		Work on these dugouts is extremely difficult, the frost has made excavation almost impossible. Nearly all timber and materials have to be delivered	

2353 Wt. W2544/1454 700,000 5/15 D.D. & L. A.D.S.S./Forms/C. 2118.

WAR DIARY or INTELLIGENCE SUMMARY

Army Form C. 2118.

Place	Date	Hour	Summary of Events and Information	Remarks and references to Appendices
RESERVE BATTALION SUBSECTOR	1917 FEBRUARY 15		2/Lt. evacuated sick 2/Lt. HYATT to hospital. 2/Lt. CURTIS D.C.M. evacuated sick to ENGLAND	
"	16th		Continue to supply large parties to R.E. Intends on Battalion generally except the number of men it is possible to supply.	
"	17th		122nd BRIGADE relieved by 123rd Brigade. Battalion remains in reserve at DICKEBUSCH and VOORMEZEELE. Captain. SINGLE evacuated sick to ENGLAND	
"	18th		2/Lt. GREAR E J L, wounded on the Somme, rejoins	
"	19th		Wiring party two over wiring gap between Centre and Left Battalions carrying party of 26 to take wire to LOCALITY. (Gap between battalions O 3 c 3. 7 to about O 3 c. 8. 5. 1 O R wounded. 1 O R evacuated sick.	
"	20th	3/-a.m	At Gourdin H.T.M. fires on O 3 d 4. 25	
"	21st		Officer in charge of wiring party at left of LOCALITY and in Enfant Loose. Several in attempting outpost wire already put out and wander in german gun wire up 5 yds from Lonsignet, they stay in the front trenches. Not an hour to inspect wire when enemy leaving there voices throws a volley of bombs. Both officer and 1 O R are slightly wounded but they	

Army Form C. 2118.

WAR DIARY
or
INTELLIGENCE SUMMARY.
(Erase heading not required.)

Instructions regarding War Diaries and Intelligence Summaries are contained in F.S. Regs., Part II. and the Staff Manual respectively. Title pages will be prepared in manuscript.

Place	Date	Hour	Summary of Events and Information	Remarks and references to Appendices
RESERVE	19 Jany		Succeed in crawling back through every wire, the enemy returning to release two officers from the wire three times, and in rear his S.L.A. kept at a trench. We returned to 7 Corps line at after this incident just out.	
BATTALION SECTOR	21		out of the wiring party.	
"	22		123 Brigade relieve 122nd Brigade. Battalion remains in reserve in DICKEBUSH and VOORMEZEELE covering area under the command of the 128th Brigade. In spite of continued working parties, Battalion in a whole was more adopting in excess than doing the usual working parties. VOORMEZEELE confirms agreed that they may not be relieved by DICKEBUSH companies.	
"	23		Our artillery very active most of the day. Very windy and exposed, bad weather for the registration of artillery brought up to sub timunite raid.	
"	24		Another trench mortar confirmed on the centre battalion front Code name CYRIL. 2/Lt. BEDINGHAM killed. 1 OR wounded.	0.20.83
		4.55	ZERO HOUR for raid of 10th Queens 124th Brigade on HOLLANDSCHESCHUUR REDOUBT. Demonstration on ST. ELOI Centre. Enemy opens fire on centre battalion trenches	

Army Form C. 2118.

WAR DIARY
or
INTELLIGENCE SUMMARY.
(Erase heading not required.)

Instructions regarding War Diaries and Intelligence Summaries are contained in F.S. Regs., Part II. and the Staff Manual respectively. Title pages will be prepared in manuscript.

Place	Date	Hour	Summary of Events and Information	Remarks and references to Appendices
RESERVE BATTALION SECTOR	24th	4.25	and the demonstration proved to be of much value to raiders. Major KNAPP rejoined after being wounded on the Somme.	
"	25th		The retaliation by the enemy during demonstration along front line and for 70 odd yards back. Barrage particularly intense at LOCALITY track leading back to OLD FRENCH TRENCH, and at dugout line behind MIDPATCH. SHELLY LANE heavily shelled, but CONVENT LANE and the R. Line received very little attention.	
"	26th	3/-	41st Divisional Artillery shell OBEY TRENCH at 0.75 and 0.20. 1 OR wounded. Wiring party now engaged on thickening wire around CASTLE MOUND FORT	
"	27th		122nd Brigade relieve 123rd Brigade. Relieve starts at 1.30 p.m instead of usual time of 9.30 a.m. Battalion remains in reserve (coming under the command of G.O.C. 122 Brigade)	
"	28th		Relieved by 18th K.R.R. 1st Platoon coming up at 10.30 a.m. Battalion marches to rest at CHIPPEW. CAMP.	

Alan B Haig Bn
Lieut Col. O/C O3rd Rifle

Army Form C. 2118

23rd Middlesex Regt

WAR DIARY
or INTELLIGENCE SUMMARY
(Erase heading not required.)

Vol XI

for the Month of MARCH 1917.

Place	Date	Hour	Summary of Events and Information	Remarks and references to Appendices
CHIPPEWA CAMP RENINGHELST	1917 MARCH 1st		Range 16 allotted to us for half the Battalion. Range 15 however unfit for use. Half Battalion left at CHIPPEWA Baths. Companies check deficiencies. Box respirator drill and bayonet fighting. Contact work between signallers and aeroplane, with 11 OR enemies? with	
"	2nd		Remainder of battalion go to CHIPPEWA Baths. 100 OR go to Brigade school for days training. Lewis Gun Officers and N.C.Os attend Armourer demonstration. 3 OR evacuated sick	
"	3rd		Training in Musketry, Battalion Drill. Half holiday granted. Football matches Brigade Commander visits camp and inspects battalion in Box respirator drill. Battalion contest.	
"	4th		Whole Battalion employed on making fascines. 1 OR evacuated sick. Brigade hand flags in the evening.	
CENTRE BATTN SUB-SECTOR	5th		Relieved 15 Hants in centre battalion outposts	
"	6th	3/- m -4 A.m	Medium French Mortars cut wire in front of the craters. Garrison of Right front Company reduced during operation 1 OR wounded, 1 OR evacuated sick with measles.	
"	7th	3.45 - 3.30/m	Medium French Mortars cut wire in front of the craters. 2 Lt FOSTER evacuated sick, 1 OR evacuated sick, 1 OR wounded	
		9 A.m.	21st Company relief. Set of Mills new type of equipment sent to us for trial	

WAR DIARY
or
INTELLIGENCE SUMMARY

(Erase heading not required.)

Army Form C. 2118

Place	Date	Hour	Summary of Events and Information	Remarks and references to Appendices
CENTRE BATT'N SUB-SECTOR ST. ELOI	MARCH 7th		Yeomen Camer across No MAN'S LAND and is addled by the regiment.	
"	8th		Enemy raid on 16th Division. Battalion warned that it may have to stand to.	
"	9th	1.30pm to 2.15	Medium French Mortars cut wire in front of Centre.	
"	10th		Chief work in line Consists of reconstruction of VOORMEZEELE SWITCH. 1 OR killed. 1 OR wounded. 1 OR evacuated sick.	
CHIPPEWA CAMP	11th		Very few men have been available for work this tour owing to very large R.E. parties to be supplied. Battalion returns to CHIPPEWA CAMP. Relieved by 18th K.R.R's.	
"	12th		A hundred men loaned to Brigade school for a day's training. Brigadier held conference with C.Os. 3 OR evacuated sick. Brigade began to train 16 workmen as Leaders.	
"	13th		Companies check deficiencies. Musketry training and Battalion drill.	
"	14th		Battalion employed on working parties. 1 OR evacuated P.B.	
"	15th		Battn. goes to CHIPPEWA Bath. Attack practice by companies. Training of workmen continues.	

WAR DIARY
or
INTELLIGENCE SUMMARY

(Erase heading not required.)

Army Form C. 2118

Place	Date	Hour	Summary of Events and Information	Remarks and references to Appendices
CHIPPEWA CAMP.	16th		A hundred men go to Brigade School for a days training. Lt. Johnson and 2 Lt. NORRIS appointed acting Captains.	
Reserve Sector.	17th		Relieved 15th HANTS in DICKEBUSCH, VOORMEZEELE, and ECLUSE TRENCH. Proportions 2 Companies and H.Q. in DICKEBUSCH, 1 Company VOORMEZEELE, 1 Company in ECLUSE TRENCH.	
"	18th		VOORMEZEELE Company employed when possible in building dugouts in McGEE TRENCH, MIDDLESEX LANE, and VOORMEZEELE SWITCH. 2 OR wounded.	
"	19th		Duffy's very large party for R.E. Every man used. 1 OR evacuated sick.	
"	20th		Wiring parties sent to Right Battalion Subsector to wire mine shafts. Wiring continues from dusk to dawn.	
"	21st		Most of men earmarked for dugout construction are being taken for R.E. parties. 2 OR evacuated sick.	
"	22nd		During mornings Platoon Sgts. attend lectures on Lewis Gun tactics. Training of Lewis Gun men and Scouts also continue in reserve Billets.	

Army Form C. 2118

WAR DIARY
or
INTELLIGENCE SUMMARY
(Erase heading not required.)

Instructions regarding War Diaries and Intelligence Summaries are contained in F.S. Regs., Part II. and the Staff Manual respectively. Title Pages will be prepared in manuscript.

Place	Date	Hour	Summary of Events and Information	Remarks and references to Appendices
CHIPPEWA CAMP.	23rd		Relieved by 18th K.R.R. in reserve sector. Battalion returns to CHIPPEWA CAMP. 2Lt BAINES G. transferred to R.F.C. 2Lt GORE wounded. 1 OR wounded. 2Lt PRIOR G joins. C	
"	24th	7.40 p.m.	Artillery activity heard. Stand to ordered.	
		8.10 p.m.	Stand down ordered	
		M(idnight)	Enemy raided N. and S. of Canal. Adopt summer time	
"	25th		Most of battalion employed on working parties. 2 OR evacuated sick. Distribution of medal ribbons by Divisional Commander to 123rd Brigade. No. 83562 A/Sgt TURNER awarded military medal. 2Lt GORE died of wounds.	
"	26th		150 OR inoculated. CHIPPEWA BATHS allotted to Battn. 2Lt MARK F.T. and 2Lt McGUIRE R.B. join	
"	27th		50 OR inoculated. 100 OR attend Brigade School for day's training. C.O attends Lewis trazen Course	

Army Form C. 2118

WAR DIARY
or
INTELLIGENCE SUMMARY
(Erase heading not required.)

Instructions regarding War Diaries and Intelligence Summaries are contained in F.S. Regs, Part II. and the Staff Manual respectively. Title Pages will be prepared in manuscript.

Place	Date	Hour	Summary of Events and Information	Remarks and references to Appendices
CHIPPEWA CAMP.	28th		Training in attack practice by Companies. Battalion drill and musketry training.	
"	29th		Battalion employed on working parties for R.E. Capt. SAYER A/ and 2 Lt Thompson S.O. join the regiment.	
CENTRE BATTN. 30th SUBSECTOR	30th		Relieve 15th HANTS in centre Battalion subsector. First platoon in DICKEBUSCH 9.30 a.m.	
"	31st	9.45 –10.5	Medium trench mortars cut mine offensite O.31 No gas reported in enemy wine offsite craters. Sent out patrols both from night and left front line companies to investigate damage to enemy wine in front of craters and Shells. Wine in front of No 5 crater has not been cut. Wine in front of No. 2 and 3 craters well cut. A warning of gas related by Battalion on left. Enemy also reported sounding gas alarms	

Alan R Hargreaves
Lieut Col
O.C. 22nd R. Liv.

WAR DIARY or INTELLIGENCE SUMMARY

Army Form C. 2118.

23 Middlesex Regt
Vol 12

Place	Date	Hour	Summary of Events and Information	Remarks and references to Appendices
CENTRE BATTALION SUBSECTOR	1917 APRIL 1st		Battalion trench strength 518 OR. Enemy artillery very active on back areas. Particularly random field guns. Enemy raid eminently probably in BLUFF sector. 1 OR killed. 1 OR wounded accidentally. 2 evacuated sick.	
"	2nd		Enemy patrol seen to approach LOCALITY during night. Dispersed by Lewis Gun fire. Signs of preparation for offensive action in our subsector noticed. Working parties of R.F.A. commence to building gun emplacements at junction of CONVENT LANE and the BOLLAART BEEK. Dugouts R.A.M.C. also working party REGIMT. STRETCHERS making themselves.	
"	3rd	9pm –9.30pm	M.T.M's out wire in front of Gaters. Enemy retaliates on CONVENT and SHELLEY LANES and also one beach on front line. Working party has to work all night to clear communication trenches so that they may be practice for the coming relief. Enemy patrol seen to approach locality and so dispersed by Lewis gun fire. 1 OR killed. 2Lt. ABBOTT returned off strength.	
"	4th		During the early morning a fighting patrol was sent out from the locality to attempt to catch the patrol that has visited us on previous nights given enemy. No enemy patrol seen.	

Army Form C. 2118.

WAR DIARY
or
INTELLIGENCE SUMMARY.
(Erase heading not required.)

Instructions regarding War Diaries and Intelligence Summaries are contained in F. S. Regs., Part II. and the Staff Manual respectively. Title pages will be prepared in manuscript.

Place	Date	Hour	Summary of Events and Information	Remarks and references to Appendices
	1917			
CENTRE BATTALION SUBSECTOR	APRIL 5		Relieved by 18 R.R. Battalion returns to CHIPPEWA CAMP. On return 200 O.R. not inoculated. These are to remain behind when the battalion marches to its training area and to travel by train. 2/Lt FORSTER H.W.B. evacuated sick. 1 O.R. evacuated sick.	Reference 11/10 H.428 BROWN S.A.
CHIPPEWA CAMP	6th		Start 3 days march to GANSPETTE training area. Battalion marches off at 9 a.m. and marches via ABEELE to cross roads before the 7 kilometre mark on the POPERINGHE – STEENVOORDE Road. Billeting party met battalion here and billets are established on farms between GODEWAERSVELDE and the STEENVOORDE – ABEELE road. Battalion in billets by 1.15 p.m.	
GODEWAERS VELDE	7th		Battalion continues its march via STEENVOORDE – CASSEL to ARNEKE. Battalion marches in threes instead of in fours. Transport and mackes separately from battalion. Billets established in ARNEKE by 2 p.m.	11
ARNEKE	8th		123rd Brigade marching as a brigade completes its march via MENEGAT – LEDERZEELE STA. – WATTEN – GANSPETTE to RAVENSHEM LES EPERLECQUES. Established in billets 4.45 p.m. No men fell out during 3 days march.	

2353 Wt. W2344/1454 700,000 5/15 D. D. & L. A.D.S.S./Forms/C.2118.

Army Form C. 2118.

WAR DIARY
or
INTELLIGENCE SUMMARY.
(Erase heading not required.)

Place	Date	Hour	Summary of Events and Information	Remarks and references to Appendices
BAYENGHEM	1917 APRIL 9th		Reorganisation of Platoons and checking of deficiencies.	
L.ES 2 PERNES GUES				
"	10th		One hour drill. Lewis Gun training and Tom bury. 1 OR evacuated sick	
"	11th		Firing on full size range. Companies in attack formation. 1 OR evacuated sick	
"	12th		Many men who have been detached from battalion for months have rejoined battalion for training. Parade strength increased as 727 OR. Lecture to all officers and N.C.Os at 4.15 p.m. by C.O.	
"	13th		The weather is hampering training considerably. Training impossible today after dinner down. Men employed at leisure.	
"	14th		Companies practice the attack during the morning. Half holiday granted etc.	
"	15th		Sunday. Battalion granted a day's holiday.	
"	16th		The day has been too wet and cold for serious training and it is found best to return to billets from training area before the dinner hour.	

WAR DIARY
or
INTELLIGENCE SUMMARY

Place	Date	Hour	Summary of Events and Information	Remarks and references to Appendices
RAVENSBERG LES EPERLECQUES	1917 APRIL 16		MAJOR KNAPP lectures to all officers and N.C.Os.	
"	17		Battalion attack practice in marked out ground representing the trenches proposed to attack. Battalion frontage OASIS STREET (inclusive) to OAR AVENUE (exclusive) Pheasant 9 WT SEW.IP 1st Objective RED LINE now support line in continuation of OAR SUPPORT TRE. 35 W.2 2nd Objective GREEN LINE DAMM STRASSE 1/10,000 3rd Final Objective BLUE LINE running through PHEASANT WOOD 200 yds in front of green line.	
"	18		2Lt PORTER R.A. and 2Lt SALTER C.L. join. 2Lt HYATT M.P. struck off strength unfit to return	
"	19		Brigade attack practice in Divisional Commanders present. Division Order attached.	
"	20		Brigade attack practice Army Commander present	
"	21		Brigade attack practice Corps Commander present	
"	22		Day's holiday granted. Reinforcement 3 OR	
"	23		Moved as Vanguard of Brigade as advance guard from BAYENGHEM LES Reference EPERLECQUES to ARNEKE via WATTEN—WULVER DINGHE — LEDERZEELE — HAZEBROUCK MENEGAT. D OR Enumerated D.R. 5. A.	

Army Form C. 2118.

WAR DIARY
or
INTELLIGENCE SUMMARY.
(Erase heading not required.)

Instructions regarding War Diaries and Intelligence Summaries are contained in F. S. Regs., Part II. and the Staff Manual respectively. Title pages will be prepared in manuscript.

Place	Date	Hour	Summary of Events and Information	Remarks and references to Appendices
ARNEKE	1917 APRIL 24th		March from ARNEKE to same billets near GODWAERSVELDE as occupied on first night of march to training area. Route ARNEKE — CASSEL — STEENVOORDE — GODWAERSVELDE	Reference HAZEBROUCK 5A.
GODWAERS VELDE	25th		March from GODWAERSVELDE to RENINGHELST VIA ABEELE to INN near 1 Km. mark on POPERINGHE STEENVOORDE ROAD and from there by a new road on to the POPERINGHE RENINGHELST ROAD. Return to CHIPPEWA CAMP. Only two her(?) (ill) fails to stand the three days march — (36 Ranks)	
CHIPPEWA CAMP	26		Large number of men are again to detached from Battalion for other branches of the Service.	
RENINGHELST	27th		Training by Companies. Battalion supplies large R.E. Working Parties.	
"	28th		Company training.	
"	29th			
"	30		Training in Limbing and Lewis gun work. 2 Lt MGUIRE R.B. accidentally killed. 2 OR wounded. Battalion parade strength 596.	

Alan Richardson Lieut Col
O.C. 23rd Midds.

ORDERS FOR TOMORROW'S OPERATIONS BY LIEUT.COLONEL A.R. HAIG-BROWN COMMANDING 23rd BATTALION MIDDLESEX REGIMENT.

Issued as an appendix to 123rd Infantry Brigade Practice O.O. No.O./5.

---oOo---

1. The Battalion will attack on a frontage of 250 yards: C and A Companies (C on the right) will divide this frontage between them: B Company will be in support of C Company and D Company in support of A Company.

2. Each Company will be in three waves each wave consisting of a platoon.

3. There will be 100 yards distance between each wave.

4. Attached to second wave will be half a platoon of D.L.I. to mop up enemy's front line. Attached to third wave will be half a platoon of D.L.I. to mop up enemy support line.

5. The mopping up of the DAMSTRASSE will be done by the Middlesex sixth wave, e.g., the rear platoons of B and D Companies.

6. Behind the Middlesex final wave will come two *skeleton* platoons of D.L.I. which will form a seventh wave and remain in enemy support line. One platoon of D.L.I. will form the eighth wave and will stay in *skeleton* enemy's front line.

7. The Middlesex Pioneers under Lieut. Mark will form the ninth wave and will proceed to the DAMSTRASSE line which they will consolidate.

8. The fifth wave, e.g., the second platoon of B and D Companies will provide all carriers.

9. Two Vickers Guns will move with the second wave and two with Battalion H.Q.
The Stokes Gun will move with Battalion H.Q.

10. The Dressing Station will move with Battalion H.Q. till it reaches the enemy support line where it will be established.

11. Zero hour will be 10.30 a.m. Watches will be synchronised at 10 a.m. on the ground.

12. Battalion H.Q. will follow in rear of the ninth wave conforming to the movements of the Battalion. All reports to be sent there.

15. 4. 17.

Geo B Smith
Lieut.,
A/Adjutant,
23rd Middlesex Regiment.

NOTES FOR TOMORROW's OPERATIONS by LIEUT. COL. A.R. Haig-Brown, Commanding 23rd Middlesex Regiment.
----

1. Zero hour will be 10.30 a.m..

2. An hour before zero, the Battalion will have closed up so that there is 30 yards between waves and 15 yards between lines.

3. Order of Attack:-

    A   ↑   C
    D   B

    (Each Company in three waves)

    Pioneers.

    Battn. H.Q.

4. At Z - 11, the whole Battalion will move forward until the leading line of the leading wave is 80 yards from the barrage and then lie down.

5. At Z plus 4, barrage lifts - First waves (the two lines of each merged) assault enemy's front line - cross it and conform again to barrage.

6. At Z plus 15, barrage lifts off enemy's Support Line and remains stationary 200 yards forward of it - First waves assault - cross trench and advance to within 80 yards of barrage.

7. At Z plus 35, barrage starts to creep - all troops follow at 80 yards distance, barrage halts on Green Line (DAMSTRASSE) and all troops lie down till Z plus 59, when troops assault.

8. At this point, 1, 2 and 3 waves remain to mop up DAMSTRASSE. No.4 wave pushes on to consolidate Blue Line. No. 5 wave remains to help mop up DAMSTRASSE and then proceeds to Blue Line. No. 6 wave pushes straight on to help No. 4 consolidate Blue Line.
No. 4 and No. 6 waves push out advanced post and patrols. The Pioneers push forward and join in the consolidation of the Blue line.
N.B. No. 5 is also the carrying wave but is to drop its stores in the enemy Support Line.

9. Moppers-up from D.L.I. will accompany 2nd and 3rd waves (on the left in each case)- they will mop up enemy support and front line and remain there.

10. 2 Vickers Guns will move on the right of the 2nd and 3rd waves respectively and two will move on the right of Battn. H.Q.

11. The Stokes Guns will move with Battn. H.Q. and will take up a position in the consolidated Blue Line.

18. 4. 17.   Alan R Haig Brown. Lieut. Colonel
                              Commanding 23rd Middlesex Regiment.

WAR DIARY MAY 1917 23 Middlesex

Army Form C. 2118

INTELLIGENCE SUMMARY

23 Middlesex

WO/13

Place	Date	Hour	Summary of Events and Information	Remarks and references to Appendices
CHIPPEWA CAMP RENINGHELST	MAY 1st		Total Strength 40 Officers 935 O.R. Trench Strength 19 Officers 547 O.R. Relieved 32nd R.F. 12th Brigade Right Subsector (trenches O11 – O24 inclusive)	
Right subsector ST. ELOI	2nd		First platoon arrived in DICKEBUSCH at 9 a.m. Relief complete 12.30 pm 10th R.W.K. on Left. 16th Division on right.	
		9.30 pm	Gas Alarm. Stromboli sounded an arm left. Our front line was not taken warning up, but kept very alert. German gas attack on our Enemy's recent raid has left the centre of our front line in a very bad condition. Wire around mine shaft in S.14, and No 1 CRATER has been badly damaged. No 1 CRATER is no longer to be manned by day, as owing to the ardent condition of the trench it can be commanded from the trench by a Lewis gun. It is to be manned at night by a listening post.	
	3rd			
	4th		The very fine mist that we left at our disposal are employed in strengthening the wire round the mine shaft, and to the left of NO 1 CRATER. Bombing gates were also erected in communication trenches near the mine. 1 Killed 5 Wounded.	

Army Form C. 2118.

WAR DIARY
or
INTELLIGENCE SUMMARY

MAY 1917

(Erase heading not required.)

Place	Date	Hour	Summary of Events and Information	Remarks and references to Appendices
Right subsector ST. ELOI	MAY 5th		C.S.M. JENNINGS appointed to commission 27th in this Battalion. We are asked to supply 230 men on R.E. fatigue. 153 as a cover to	
-"-	6th	10 pm	Company in R. Line relieves Company that garrison the mine shaft and front line between MIDDLESEX LANE and CONVENT LANE. Company in MIDDLESEX LANE relieves Company in Right front line (O.1.1, O.1.2, O.2.1.)	
-"-	7th	9 pm	During for the 8th night in succession heavy bombardment on back areas in retaliation for our repeated shots on the "DAMM" STRASSE, etc. BRASSERIE receives attention. I warned.	
-"-	8th	9.10pm - 9.15pm	Heavy bombardment in retaliation for hostile activity on our back areas. Every gun and how on Second Army front fires at an intense rate on enemy communications, lines, enemy back fire as sound as our back area. Capt W.E.A. Harrison Lt. R.A.M.C. on mine practice repeats. I evacuated sick	
-"-		11-15pm - 11.30	On our having each day for a week commencing 5th Telephone communication broken down to rest a remain north of Communication last manage pent by Visual and Runner.	

2353 Wt. W2544/1454 700,000 5/15 D.D.&L. A.D.S.S. Forms/C. 2118.

Army Form C. 2118.

WAR DIARY
or
INTELLIGENCE SUMMARY.

MAY 1917

(Erase heading not required.)

Place	Date	Hour	Summary of Events and Information	Remarks and references to Appendices
Right subsection ST.ELOI	9th cont 9th	9.15p.m	Battalion Relay Runner Post established at junction of P.o.B. Trench and R. Line, and at junction of MIDDLESEX LANE and R. Line. Enemy opens heavy artillery fire on front line, R. Line, S.14 communication trenches and even round Battalion H.Q. Red lights seen to go up on our right. Every man stands to. After a time our guns answer.	
—		10.30p.m.	Our guns cease firing. Right front company received more attention than left front company. Right front line, S.14, R. Line, are shelled heavily, but incessantly. No damage was done to these trenches, except in R. Line between CRATER LANE and BUS HOUSE. P.O trench a breach in 8 places. MIDDLESEX LANE & 2 Avn Webs cut Communication held good until about the last enemy shell when the left front line became "dis". No casualties by shell fire. 1 O.R. killed by bullet. Parties sent out to retain communication trenches.	

Army Form C. 2118.

WAR DIARY
or
INTELLIGENCE SUMMARY.
(Erase heading not required.)

May 1917

Place	Date	Hour	Summary of Events and Information	Remarks and references to Appendices
Right sub sector ST. ELOI	MAY 10th	10	Relief of Brigade by 124 Brigade arranged for tomorrow. We effect to be relieved by 10th Queens. Orders are sent out. Relief is cancelled in the evening.	
—	11th		In spite of the shortage of men at the disposal of the battalion for carrying parties and mining parties we have put out 552 coils of wire for front line and for mine shaft defences. 18 R.W.Ks take over H4th Div trenches up to 36/39. 1 wounded.	
HQ. + 2 Coys: DICKEBUSH HUTS 1 Coy: Mic Mac Camp 1 Coy: GHQ Line	12th		Relieved in front line system by 20 D.L.I, and move into reserve. Relief over by 3 p.m. Our garrison of front line has to return to take over tunnels and start out again without rest on an R E working party. Dispositions in reserve co: 1 Company in G.H.Q 2 sound lines. 2 Companies Orrd Batt. H.Q. 2 in dugouts behind bank of Dickebush Stang. 1 Company in Mic Mac Camp.	
—	13th		Battalion on working parties. Officers and N.C.O's commence nightly reconnaissance of the Battalion assembly ground.	
—	14th		Working parties and Reconnaissance continue. 1 wounded	

WAR DIARY or INTELLIGENCE SUMMARY

Army Form C. 2118.

May 1917

Place	Date	Hour	Summary of Events and Information	Remarks and references to Appendices
	MAY			
As over	15		Battalion on Working Parties for R.E. & other work out to the Battalion began having which had been on Breckhurst Lake for 2 years all drawn to refit.	
—	16.		Working Parties as usual	
—	17.		2nd L.T. sent out strong patrol. Much German trenches searched thoroughly but no prisoner taken. Patrol out from 10 p.m. till 3 a.m.	
—	18.		2nd L.T. failed to get in German trenches from 10 p.m. to midnight	
—	19.		Working Parties	
ALBERTA CAMP RENINGHELST	20		Relieved by 11 R.W.R. Working parties. One gallant patrol E. ALBERTA. 16 reinforcements. 1 killed, 6 wounded, sick.	
—	21.		Working Parties. 2/T Bilbrough to Tampier.	
—	22		Working Parties. We are reinforced by G.R.O.T.R. Classified as Trained. Maj Knapp appointed to command 12 E. Surreys.	
—	23		Working Parties.	
—	24		Working Parties. Baths allotted but impossible to bath all men because of day Working Parties.	
—	25th		C.O. proceeds to GAYSPETTE to confer with 12th Bde about the offensive	

Army Form C. 2118.

WAR DIARY
or
INTELLIGENCE SUMMARY.

(Erase heading not required.)

May 1917

Instructions regarding War Diaries and Intelligence Summaries are contained in F. S. Regs., Part II. and the Staff Manual respectively. Title pages will be prepared in manuscript.

Place	Date	Hour	Summary of Events and Information	Remarks and references to Appendices
ALBERTA CAMP	MAY 25th (cont)		He returns at 3 p.m. Brigade Horse Show.	
REINING HEBST	26th		Relieved 12 E. Surrey in Right Subsector - relief complete at 12.30 p.m. 180 men arrive late owing to 60 hiking party. 1 Killed.	
Right Subsector ST ELOI	27th	2 a.m.	Small mine blown opposite trench O.26. Believed successful. No enemy action followed. Enemy commenced formation of advanced Battalion dumps for offensive. 1 Killed, 4 wounded	
"		9 p.m.	Enemy opened fire all calibres on sector. Shelling continued round VOORMEZEELE	
"	28 - 9 3 a.m.		Bde area. Apparently hostile round VOORMEZEELE.	
"		2 a.m.	Gas alarm sounded on left. Author not known. Alarm false. Believed to have originated through enemy using gas shells in his bombardment. Work on dumps continues though vicinity is badly shelled. 2 wounded. 4 Killed.	
"		9 p.m.	Enemy again opened fire on sector. Gun blown out and ammunition dump exploded near Batt H.Q. 2. 38 Reinforcements.	
"	29th		Morning exceptionally quiet. Sector visited by H.R.H The Prince of Wales. Afternoon some shelling. Night, 51 Brigade on our immediate right.	

Army Form C. 2118.

WAR DIARY
or
INTELLIGENCE SUMMARY.

(Erase heading not required.)

Instructions regarding War Diaries and Intelligence Summaries are contained in F. S. Regs., Part II. and the Staff Manual respectively. Title pages will be prepared in manuscript.

Place	Date	Hour	Summary of Events and Information	Remarks and references to Appendices
Right subsector ST.ELOI	29th	cont.	relieved by 56th Brigade (19th Div).	
— " —	30.	2.a.m	20.A.L.9 Attempt raid opposite our right front with artillery preparation. 3.a.m made it good failing. Casualties to them 1 wounded. 1 injured by mine.	
— " —		11.30 a.m.	Practice Barrage opposite Battalion front. Results apparent most satisfactory. Heavies continue on enemy internuncio area. Work on dumps. Relieved by 11 R.W.K. Came back to CHIPPEWA B.	
CHIPPEWA CAMP. RENINGHELST.	31st		Total Strength. 40 officers 994 other ranks. Trench Strength 31 officers 551 other ranks.	

Alex R Taylor Lieut. Colonel
Commanding 23rd Middlesex Regt.

23 Middlesex Regt.

Army Form C. 2118

WAR DIARY
or
INTELLIGENCE SUMMARY
(Erase heading not required.)

Place	Date	Hour	Summary of Events and Information	Remarks and references to Appendices
Chippawa Camp.	June 1st		Deficiencies checked. Maj. E Knapp posted to command the 12th East Surrey Regt. Three evac. Sick.	
	2nd		Chippawa Baths allotted to the Battalion.	
	3rd		Battalion practice relieving up and the advancing. 10 R. evacuated Sick.	
	4th		Battalion by Companies train in the show advance needed behind the Barrage.	
	5th		X Day.	
		10am	One Company starts from Chippawa Camp and proceed by overland route to take over trenches prior to assembly. Take over OLD FRENCH TRENCH RIGHT of CONVENT LANE.	
		10pm	Remaining three Companies march to trench and take over as follows :— 1 Platoon GORDON LANE, 5 Platoons in VOORHEZEELE SWITCH, 1 Coy in Old FRENCH TRENCH, H.qrs in OLD FRENCH TRENCH. Enemy shell with Gas shells on route. Water for Y clay drawn on route	
		10pm	One Platoon proceed to locality. Cut our wire, make steps in parapet and out patrol which reports ENEMY'S FRONT LINE lightly held. 10 R. evacuated Sick.	

Army Form C. 2118

WAR DIARY
or
INTELLIGENCE SUMMARY
(Erase heading not required.)

Instructions regarding War Diaries and Intelligence Summaries are contained in F. S. Regs., Part II. and the Staff Manual respectively. Title Pages will be prepared in manuscript.

Place	Date	Hour	Summary of Events and Information	Remarks and references to Appendices
Left Sector.	June 6th	6am	Y day. Rations and water for 2 days drawn from the G.H.Q Line dump, and S.A.A., Bombs and Very lights from the Convent Lane dump.	
		10pm	Everything remain quiet until about 10pm when the Enemy started opening fire with his Field Guns on VOORMEZEELE SWITCH, OLD FRENCH TRENCH, and the place of Assembly	
		10:30pm	Lt. PURVES killed whilst preparing the assembly ground at 10.30pm.	
		M.M. 11-12.0	Coy moved up to place of Assembly by means of platoons. Slight shelling. 10R Covered Lick	
Assembly Ground.	7th	3.10am	Zero hour. Trench Strength 16 officers 550 O.R.	
		2.30am	Battalion in Six waves in position on assembly ground.	
		2.45am	Battalion move forward to within 70 yds of the Enemy's line.	
		3.5am	Observed a golden rain rocket fired from RUINED FARM, threatened to give away our assembly position, but no action followed.	
		3.7am	The Mine in No 3 Crater goes up at the same time an Artillery crop barrage on Enemy's	
FRONT LINE.		3.10am	Battalion move forward and the barrage jumps to support trench	

Army Form C. 2118

WAR DIARY
or
INTELLIGENCE SUMMARY
(Erase heading not required.)

Place	Date	Hour	Summary of Events and Information	Remarks and references to Appendices
Ploune	June 7th		The Battalion found great difficulty in keeping touch with the battalions on our flanks owing to the smoke and dust caused by our own artillery. Casualties:-	4 Off. Killed 6 wounded. O.R. 26 Killed 215 wounded 5 missing
Daurnstrasse		4.5am	Daurnstrasse stormed and captured, 80 prisoners taken.	
			Advanced posts pushed out about 80 yds in front of Daurnstrasse. Consolidate a line about 50yds South of the Daurnstrasse. Most of our casualties occur near the Enemy's Support Line	
		6.30am	122nd Brigade leapfrog us and Capture Blackline, followed by Tank.	
		4.30am to 6 pm	Work of consolidation continues. Slight shelling.	
		2.4pm	24th Division leapfrog the Battalion and advance to the Green line.	
		10pm	Rations and water arrive for 'A' day.	
	8th		A day.	
		3am	Battalion relieve the 32nd Royal Fusiliers on our right. New line consolidated through Damm Wood and Pheasant Wood. Sheet 28 S.W. O9c 30.55 – O9c 9090.	
		7.30pm	Battalion move from dugout in Daurnstrasse to shell hole a few yards in rear of Blauline as it was thought probable the Daurnstrasse might be blown up. Sheet 28 S.W. O9.c.45.63.	
		10pm	Rations and water arrive for 'B' day.	

Army Form C. 2118.

WAR DIARY
or
INTELLIGENCE SUMMARY.
(Erase heading not required.)

Place	Date	Hour	Summary of Events and Information	Remarks and references to Appendices
Blue Line	June 8th	10pm	Enemy attempts assemble for counter-attack. Our artillery opens fire on Enemy assembly ground, and drops barrage.	
		11.45pm	Resume ordinary Conditions. 1 OR Evacuated Sick.	
	9th		"B" Day. Work of Consolidation Continues. During the day work is put out in front of the BLOCK LINE. Emergency ration dump formed by DOTTY WOOD. Battlefield cleared of Dead and Material.	
		7.30pm	Drumfires and Woods in vicinity constantly shelled. Enemy enfilades the BLUE LINE from the Salient but no Casualties. Night calm. Two O.R. Evacuated Sick.	
	10th		Enemy artillery again very active. He devotes his attention to the ground forward of our position.	

Instructions regarding War Diaries and Intelligence Summaries are contained in F. S. Regs., Part II. and the Staff Manual respectively. Title pages will be prepared in manuscript.

Army Form C. 2118.

WAR DIARY
or
INTELLIGENCE SUMMARY.
(Erase heading not required.)

Instructions regarding War Diaries and Intelligence Summaries are contained in F.S. Regs., Part II. and the Staff Manual respectively. Title pages will be prepared in manuscript.

Place	Date	Hour	Summary of Events and Information	Remarks and references to Appendices
Blue Line	June 10th	10pm	The enemy again unfined our position from the left. Work of consolidation continues. Parapet and firesteps receive special attention. During the day more wire is put out in front of our position. Enemy artillery active on our Front Line, is answered by our artillery opening fire.	
		11.45pm	This continues till 11.30pm. Everything again normal. One Evacuated Sick and One O.R. Wounded.	
	11th	6pm	Consolidation of our position continues. Battalion is relieved by a Company of the 26th Royal Fusiliers.	
		7.30pm	Relief complete by 7.30pm. Battalion returns to OLD FRENCH TRENCH, and takes up its position to the right of the BUS HOUSE.	
		8.30pm	Battalion back in rest in Old Reserve Line. Casualties Two O.R. Wounded. Trench Strength 8 off. & 298 O.R.	

Army Form C. 2118

Instructions regarding War Diaries and Intelligence Summaries are contained in F.S. Regs, Part II. and the Staff Manual respectively. Title Pages will be prepared in manuscript.

WAR DIARY
or
INTELLIGENCE SUMMARY
(Erase heading not required.)

Place	Date	Hour	Summary of Events and Information	Remarks and references to Appendices
RESERVE LINE	June 13th		Men rest. Deficiencies checked. Casualties { O.R: 3 Wounded, 1 Evacuated Sick. }	
	13th	2–6 pm	Battalion allowed the use of the baths at ELZENWALLE CHATEAU.	
	14th		Battalion supplies working parties for salvage work. O.R. = 2 Evacuated Sick.	
	15th		The Battalion unable to obtain much rest owing to our own gun fire.	
	16th		Reorganisation and instruction of Specialists. Casualties O.R. 1 Wounded – 1 Killed	
	17th	2–6 pm	Brigade Band gives demonstration in the field between Elzenwalle Chateau and Scottish Wood	
	18th		Ditto. Casualties:- O.R: 1 Wounded.	
	19th		Battalion allowed vis-a-vis of Batts of Elzenwalle Chateau {O11a 3.5 – O5c 9.10} at Sheet 28 S.W. {O3d 9.2 – O4c 5.8} {O10b 3.7 – O5c 95.10} [BLACK SUPPORT] [BLACK] & [GREEN] lines. New Battalion	
		8 pm	Battalion relieves 15" Batts in OAK SUPPORT. Hqrs. established at O3d 95.65 as the WHITE CHATEAU, which has been consistently shelled since 2 day, is considered unsuitable.	
		11.30 pm	Relief complete by 11.30 pm.	
	20th	3 am	At dawn Enemy aeroplane flies slowly following our trench, at a low altitude firing his machine gun. Our Lewis guns fire but few rounds. Casualties 2 O.R. Evacuated Sick	
		6 am	Enemy artillery active on BLACK LINE	
		8 pm	Construction of new support line 60 yds in front of BLACK LINE consisting of portion - fire step, and building up parapet. Communication trench dug between Oak and Black line.	
		10 pm – 2 am		

Army Form C. 2118.

WAR DIARY
INTELLIGENCE SUMMARY.
(Erase heading not required.)

Instructions regarding War Diaries and Intelligence
Summaries are contained in F. S. Regs., Part II.
and the Staff Manual respectively. Title pages
will be prepared in manuscript.

Place	Date	Hour	Summary of Events and Information	Remarks and references to Appendices
New Post Line left of Canal.	June 21st		Enemy's aeroplanes fly unmolested over our lines the whole day. Heavy shelling of the front, Black line and Dammstrasse.	
		3 pm	One enemy aircraft driven down.	
		10 pm	Inter-Company relief:- Coy in Black line relieves Coy in Green line	
		11.30 pm	Relief Complete. Casualties 1 Off. Wounded. 12 O.R. Wounded. 4 Killed. 10 O.R. Acc. Wounded.	
	22nd	2.45 pm	Retaliation by our artillery on two of the Enemy's Villages. 18lbs and 4.5 Hows employed	
		3.10 pm	Bombardment finishes. Casualties 5 O.R. Killed. 6 O.R. Wounded. Enemy's artillery less active during the day but resumes its usual activity during the night.	
	23rd		Every morning at dawn one aeroplane appears over our front line and fires his Machine gun	
		12.10 am	Our artillery Bombards OBLIQUE TRENCH.	
		2.0	Durham L. Inf. raid OBLIQUE TRENCH	
	24th	2.42 am	Our artillery drops a creeping barrage on enemy shell holes South of HOLLEBEKE. Enemy retaliates a little.	

2353 Wt. W2544/1454 700,000 5/15 D. D. & L. A.D.S.S. Forms/C. 2118.

WAR DIARY or INTELLIGENCE SUMMARY

Army Form C. 2118.

Place	Date	Hour	Summary of Events and Information	Remarks and references to Appendices
New front line left of Canal	June 24th		Enemy's aeroplanes still very active. They fly very low over our trenches. Our Lewis guns and machine guns open fire but are of little success.	
		9.30pm	1 R.W. Surrey Regt. relieve us. Coy in reserve line relieved first, then front line and support line.	
		11 pm	Relief Complete. Battalion return to Old FRENCH TRENCH taking up its position to the left of SHELLEY dump to Arundell House. Casualties 4 OR. Wounded.	
OLD FRENCH TRENCH	25th	2.45.	Our artillery drops a creeping barrage on the enemy's shellholes South of HOLLEBEKE. Old French trench slightly shelled. Enemy's artillery appears to be registering.	
		9.30am		
		3pm	Heavy shelling of our position. A & B Coy take up new positions in CONVENT LANE and SHELLEY LANE. Battalion Hqrs established in Sap at the top of Convent Lane.	
		8pm		
		9.30pm	Intense bombardment by our artillery. Casualties 7 OR Wounded 5 OR Killed.	
	26th	6am	Enemy's artillery very active. C Coy take up new position in VICTORIA STREET EAST & WEST. Remainder of day reasonably quiet. Casualties 1 OR Killed, 10 OR. Wounded	

Army Form C. 2118.

WAR DIARY
INTELLIGENCE SUMMARY.
(Erase heading not required.)

Instructions regarding War Diaries and Intelligence Summaries are contained in F. S. Regs., Part II. and the Staff Manual respectively. Title pages will be prepared in manuscript.

Place	Date	Hour	Summary of Events and Information	Remarks and references to Appendices
	June			
	27th	11am	Heavy shelling round ARUNDEL HOUSE. D Coy move to SPOIL BANK Battalion to supply three working parties for R.E.	
New front line left of Canal.	28th	9pm	We relieve the 1st R.W. Surry Regt. First platoon moves off at 8.30pm	
		11.55pm	Relief Complete.	
	29th		Enemy's aeroplanes still very active. Heavy shelling of WHITE CHATEAU AREA. Remainder of day quite normal.	
		10pm	Consolidation of Support line & front line continues.	
	30th		Enemy's artillery less active.	
		11pm	Battalion relieved by the 22nd LONDON Regt, and return to Camp M6d S.8. Casualties 2 O.R. Wounded. Trench Strength of Battalion 15 Off, 236 O.R.	

COPY No. 3.

OPERATION ORDERS BY LIEUT. COL. A.R. HAIG-BROWN
Commanding 23rd MIDDLESEX REGIMENT.

Reference Maps (Sheet 28 N.E.)
              (   ) 1/20,000.
              (Sheet 28 S.E.)

INTENTION 1. The 2nd Army will be ready to resume the offensive any day after the 31st May 1917.
The Xth Corps will attack on a front from DIKKEBUSCHVIJVER to OBSERVATORY RIDGE.
The 41st Division will be on the right, the 47th Division will be on the left of the 41st Division and the 19th Division (9th Corps) will be on the right of the 41st Division.

DISPOSITION 2. On the right, 124th Infantry Brigade and 1 section
of 41st of the 237th Field Coy. R.E.
DIVISION On the left, 123rd Infantry Brigade and one section of the 233rd Field Coy.
In Divisional Reserve, the 122nd Infantry Brigade, 228 Field Coy. R.E., 233rd Field Coy. R.E. (less 1 section) ~~and 19th Middlesex Regiment (Pioneers).~~
237 Field Coy. R.E. (less one section) and 19th Middlesex Regiment (Pioneers).

DAYS PREVIOUS 3. The attack will take place on zero day after several
to ATTACK. days preliminary bombardment. Zero day will be referred to as Z day and the preceding five days as Y, X, W, V, U. The days before U day will be known as Z - 6, Z - 7 &c. The days after Zero day as A, B, C days. The days after C day as Z plus 4, Z plus 5 etc.

DISPOSITION 4. The frontage assigned to the Brigade is from
of BRIGADE O.3.c.15.75 to O.3.b.40.80.
in ATTACK. The 23rd Middlesex Regiment will be on the right, the 10th R.W.Kent Regiment in the centre and the 11th R.W.Surrey Regiment on the left.
The 20th D.L.I. will form two waves in rear of the Brigade, will halt in the enemy front and support lines and mop them up, dig in and remain as Brigade Reserve until such time as circumstances permit them to become Divisional Reserve.

DISPOSITION 5. The 123rd Infantry Brigade will enter the line on
PREVIOUS to W/X and X/Y nights and be prepared to attack at
ATTACK. Zero hour on Z day.
C Coy. 23rd Middlesex Regiment will enter the line on W/X night and the remainder of the Battalion on X/Y night. The 23rd Middlesex will then be distributed in depth with one platoon of C Coy. in its own portion of the LOCALITY, the remainder of "C" Coy. and one platoon of A Coy. in the R Line; the remainder of A Coy. (less one platoon in GORDON STREET) and all B Coy. in VOORMEZEELE SWITCH; the whole of D Coy. in advanced G.H.Q. Line.
At two hours before Zero, the 23rd Middlesex Regiment will be in its attack assembly position which has previously been reconnoitred by all Officers and N.C.Os. and an which will be marked by strings and Notice Boards.

DISPOSITION 6. The Battalion will attack on a two-platoon frontage
OF BATTAL- and its distribution will be as follows :-
ION FOR
ATTACK.

OPERATION ORDERS   -: 2 :-

6. C Coy. on the right, A Coy. on the left, B Coy.
(Cont'd) in the rear of C Coy. D Coy. in the rear of A Coy.
Each Company will be organized on a three-platoon
basis. The Battalion will assemble in 6 waves
of two lines each, there being a distance of 20
yards between each wave and 10 yards between each
line.

LIEUT. MARK.
7. BATTALION PIONEERS. In rear of the 6th wave will
be the Battalion Pioneers under Lieut. Mark.

BOUNDARY OF ATTACK.
8. The boundaries of the 23rd Middlesex Regiment in
the attack are OASIS STREET on the right, inclusive
to OAR AVENUE on the left, exclusive.

OBJECTIVES OF ATTACK.
9. There are two objectives for the Brigade in general
and the 23rd Middlesex Regt. in particular.

(1). The Red Line, which is an imaginary
line, varying from 80 to 150 yards beyond
of the enemy S Line and which will be marked
by the nearness to which approach to our
standing barrage is possible.

(2). The Blue Line, which is the line of the
DAMMSTRASSE and in front of which a line of
Advanced Posts will be formed subject also
to the nearness to which approach is possible
to our own standing barrage.

PROCEDURE of ATTACK.
10. The 23rd Middlesex Regt. will move from its
Assembly position in time to be within 75 yards
of the enemy's front line parapet at zero hour.
At zero plus three, the Artillery will lift off
the enemy front-line and, at that moment, the
leading wave, having if possible, crawled nearer
to the enemy's parapet than it's original 75
yards, will dash to the assault, followed by the
whole Battalion. The Battalion will then move
on to the enemy Support Line, where the first wave
will halt and proceed to mop it up. This wave,
the moment the 20th D.L.I. arrive, will hand over
carefully, the work of "mopping-up" and then,
after re-organization, follow in rear of the Battalion with as little delay as possible. The 2nd,
3rd, 4th, 5th and 6th waves will continue to
advance until they reach the Red Line where they will
halt in proper order.

At Z plus 35, the standing barrage will commence to
creep forward, followed as closely as possible
by the Battalion.

At Z plus 45, the barrage reaches the DAMMSTRASSE.

In proceeding from the Red Line to the DAMMSTRASSE
the 2nd wave will remain in and mop up the new
enemy Reserve Trench and the Triangle and will
then proceed to the DAMMSTRASSE.

The 3rd, 4th, 5th and 6th, and, if present, the
first 1st wave, will continue straight forward and
assault the DAMMSTRASSE as soon as the barrage
lifts,

OPERATION ORDERS -: 2 :-

DISPOSITION
OF BATTAL-
ION FOR
ATTACK.
Continued.

6. The Battalion will attack o

OPERATION ORDERS -: 3 :-

                The 3rd, 4th and 5th waves will remain to mop up the DAMMSTRASSE and the 6th, and if present, the first wave, will push forward to consolidate the line of strong points as near to our own barrage as possible.

                The 5th wave will carry water and bombs and sandbags and will dump these materials in the enemy Support Line for collection by the D.L.I. and proceed with the rest of the Battalion. The Pioneers will proceed in rear of the Battalion and finally join the 6th wave and help in the work of consolidation.

DIRECTION OF ATTACK. 11. The right flank will direct and will move down OASIS STREET on the left-hand top corner of DAMM WOOD. An arrow shows the direction of advance on right flank of assembly position and the direction is carried forward across No Man's Land by a succession of small red and yellow flags.

BATTALION RESERVE. 12. Each Company Commander will detail one Lewis Gun to move with the Battalion Pioneers as Battalion Reserve.

ACTION OF BRIGADE ON RIGHT. 13. The 124th Infantry Brigade has detailed the 32nd Fusiliers for operations on our immediate right flank. They will accompany the 23rd Middlesex Regiment to the Red Line, where they will be leap-frogged by the 26th Fusiliers who will accompany the 23rd Middlesex to the DAMMSTRASSE and thence onwards to the line to be consolidated in front of it.

VICKERS GUNS 14. Three Vickers Guns will accompany the 23rd Middlesex Regiment to the attack. These guns with their teams of ammunition carriers, move with the last line of the last wave of the Battalion. On the DAMMSTRASSE being carried, they will establish themselves in front of it, in order to meet an enemy counter-attack, and also to form a barrage for the attack by the 122nd Brigade on the Black Line. The Vickers Gun Officer attached to the 23rd Middlesex Regiment will hold himself in readiness at any time to throw a protecting flank should the Battalion on the right or on the left be held up.

STOKES GUNS 15. One Stokes Gun will be attached to the 23rd Middlesex Regiment for the attack. It will bombard the enemy's trenches from zero to zero plus 1. and will then follow the Battalion with Battalion H.Q. details. O.C. Stokes Guns will be prepared, at any moment, under my orders to deal with any enemy strong-point which holds up the attack, with enfilade fire, and when the DAMMSTRASSE is taken, will dig in on the consolidated line so as to command the Communication Trench running from the DAMMSTRASSE to OBSCURE TRENCH through PHEASANT WOOD.

SPECIAL TASKS FOR 23rd MIDDX. 16.   (1) To construct Strong Point at O.9.a.5.5. For this, B Coy. will be responsible.
        (2) To dig a Communication Trench forward from the DAMMSTRASSE, to the new consolidated line in front of it.
        D Coy. will be responsible for this.

OPERATION ORDERS   -: 4 :-

ARMAMENT	17. Will be as laid down in 123 I.B. G 56/41 of May 17th. All Officers will carry a knobkerry in addition to a revolver and every man a shovel (instead of an entrenching tool) two sandbags and two bombs. Moppers-up will carry 6 Mills and 6 P. Bombs and only 100 rounds of ammunition.
PRELIMINARY PREPARATIONS.	18. These come under the following heads :-

(1) Preparation of the Assembly Ground and Jumping off position, including making bridges over the morass, removal of wire in rear of parados of LOCALITY, making gaps in wire in front of LOCALITY and making steps and placing ladders in parapet of LOCALITY.
This work is detailed to Lieut. Mark.

(2). DIRECTION OF ATTACK.
This work is assigned to Lieut. Purves and includes also the marking off of Assembly Ground.

(3). MAKING OF DUMPS.   Under Major Gayer.

DUMPS FOR RATIONS WATER & AMMUNITION	19. On X/Y night, troops will bring in with them rations for Y day and will draw their water for Y day at a dump which has been made at H.36.b.5.6. On Y day. Companies will draw rations and water for Z day at a dump situated in the same place as above. On Y day, Companies will draw their ammunition, bombs, shovels etc. as laid down in para 18. They will also, (where necessary) draw materials for the fifth (carrying) wave. An emergency dump for rations and water for A day will be made in the LOCALITY. An emergency dump for Bombs & Ammunition will also be made in the LOCALITY.
CONTACT AEROPLANE.	20. Every man will carry two green ground flares, which will be lit in groups of five, only when called for by an aeroplane showing a white light and sounding a Klaxon horn roughly at the following times :-

Zero plus 30.
Zero plus 1.30
Zero plus 4.30
Zero plus 5.30

It must be distinctly understood that these flares will only be lit by our most advanced troops.

REGIMENTAL AID POST.	21. The Regimental Aid Posts will be in CONVENT LANE and NEW CONVENT LANE until the enemy Black Line is reached and they will then be established in dug-outs in the Enemy Support Line.
LIAISON OFFICER	22. C Coy. will detail an Officer for liaison duty with Battalion on right and D Coy. will detail an Officer for liaison duty with Battalion on our left.
SUBSEQUENT ACTION OF SUPPORTING TROOPS.	23. The 122nd Infantry Brigade will form up in rear of the DAMMSTRASSE at zero plus three hours. At zero plus 3.40 they will form up under our standing barrage and then advance with it to assault the Black Line - OBSTACLE SWITCH - OBSCURE TRENCH - OBLONG RESERVE. At zero plus 10 hours, the 24th Division will continue the attack, making the Green Line their objective. The Green Line runs from O 10 b 7.7. to 0.16.c.5.1.
TANKS.	24. Two sections of TANKS will accompany the Brigade advance.

OPERATION ORDERS -: 5 :-

ORGANIZATION of CAPTURED GROUND

25. From Front to rear :-

    (1). A line of Advanced Posts close under standing barrage about 150 yards in front of DAMSTRASSE.

    (2). A consolidated line running MARTHNS FARM and thence about 60 yards in front of DOME HOUSE - DAMSTRASSE.

    (3). A line of strong-points in rear of DAMSTRASSE about O.8.b.5.0 - O.9.a.6.5 - O.9.b.1.9 - EIKHOF FARM - O.3.d.8.3.

BATTALION H.Q. and Reports.

26. Battalion Headquarters will move behind the Battalion Pioneers until they reach the enemy Support line where a Report centre will be formed and maintained until the same can be moved forward to the DAMSTRASSE. This will be marked by a small Red and Yellow flag and all reports will be despatched there.

                                          Alan R. Haig Brar.
                                               Lieut. Colonel.
                                  Commanding 23rd Middlesex Regiment

--------oOo--------

Copy No. 1.	Filed
Copy No. 2.	War Diary
Copy No. 3.	123rd Infy. Bde.
Copy No. 4.	122nd Infy. Bde.
Copy No. 5.	124th Infy. Bde.
Copy No. 6.	O.C. 11th Queen's Regt.
Copy No. 7.	O.C. 10th R.W.Kent Regt.
Copy No. 8.	O.C. 20th D.L.I.
Copy No. 9.	O.C. 123rd M.G.Coy.
Copy No. 10.	O.C. 123rd L.T.M.B.
Copy No. 11.	O.C. 32nd Royal Fusiliers.
Copy No. 12.	O.C. 26th Royal Fusiliers.
Copy No. 13.	O.C. A Coy.
Copy No. 14.	O.C. B Coy.
Copy No. 15.	O.C. C Coy.
Copy No. 16.	O.C. D Coy.
Copy No. 17.	O.C. H.Q. Coy.
Copy No. 18.	

--------oOo--------

41st Division. A.

Herewith War Diary of 23rd Middlesex Regt. for month of July.

23rd August 1917.

Brigadier-General,
Commanding 123rd Infantry Brigade.

WAR DIARY for month of July 1917

Army Form C. 2118

23rd Battalion Middlesex Regt.

INTELLIGENCE SUMMARY

(Erase heading not required.)

Place	Date	Hour	Summary of Events and Information	Remarks and references to Appendices
THIEUSHOUK	1st July 17	6 AM–4 PM	Battalion resting at M.b 45.0.80. 1 O.R. evacuated	
"	"	5.30 PM	Battalion moves to THIEUSHOUK	
"	"	7.30 PM	Arrives in camp at THIEUSHOUK	
"	2,3 July 17		Time spent in seeing to the interior economy of the Battalion	
"	4 July 17		Specialist Company formed of NCOs to teach them to enstruct in bombing, Lewis Guns, rifle grenades. 9 reinforcements O.R	
"	"		C.O returns from leave. Evacuated sick 5 O.R	
"	5 July 9 AM–4.30 AM		Training	
"	6 "	3 AM–8 PM	Baths at La BESACE FARM allotted to Battalion A & B Company at baths. remainder training. 10 reinforcements O.R	
"	7 "	9 AM–12 noon	Training, squad drill. Rifle exercises, gas drill. 16 reinforcements O.R	
"	"	2 PM–8 PM	Range (1 x both) at LR33 allotted for the use of the Battalion	
"	8 "		Church Parade. Evacuated sick 2 O.R.	
"	9 "	9 AM–2 PM	Attack practice on training ground near BERTHEN. Performance of CRUMPS at Battn H.Q.	
"	10 "	9 AM–12 noon	Training, bayonet fighting, squad drill, and musketry. 100 reinforcements O.R	
"	"	1.30 PM–6 PM	Baths at La. BESACE. FARM. C & D Company A & B Companies training physical exercises & bayonet drill.	
"	11 "	8.30–9.30 AM	Headquarters for baths at La BESACE. FARM.	
"	"	9.35–4.30 PM	Physical exercises, bayonet fighting, musketry, gas drill & attack practice.	

WAR DIARY or INTELLIGENCE SUMMARY.

Army Form C. 2118
23rd MX
July/17
2

(Erase heading not required.)

Place	Date	Hour	Summary of Events and Information	Remarks and references to Appendices
THIEUSHOUK	12 July 1917	3.15 PM	Divisional Commander (General Lawford) inspected the Battalion and presents medals to Officers & men of the Battalion who did distinguished work during the last attack of June 7th 1917. Evacuated with 3 O.R.	
"	13 July 1917	9 AM - 12 Noon	Bayonet fighting, squad drill & spearhead training	
"	"	2 PM - 6 PM	Heats of Battalion Sports run off. 70 Staff College, Cambridge. 23rd v. C. Livingstone	
"	"	6 PM	1st Round of Brigade Football Competition 23rd Middlesex v. 11th Queens Middlesex won 3-0.	
"	14 "	9.30 AM - 4.30 PM	Battalion Sports.	
"	"	4 PM	Officers attend General Lawford's garden party at Berthen. 3/4 H. Stevenson & 4th W. Rochart joined battalion.	
"	15 "	9 AM	Church Parade. 2 Lieuts A.S. Tilburey, J.T. Hemphrey, J.P. Rees, B. Bright, C.S. Gomlotery joined battalion.	
"	"	10 AM	New draft inspected by the Brigadier General C.W.B. Gordon.	
"	"	11 AM	Brigade Football Competition, 2nd Round. Middlesex v. 20th Durham Light Infantry Battalion thereby became the Brigade representatives in the Divisional Football Competition.	
"	"	2 PM - 7.30 PM	Brigade Sports Prizes presented to winners by the Brigadier General C.W.B. Gordon.	
"	16 "	9 AM - 10 AM	IX Corps Range at R.33.e. allotted for the use of the Battalion.	
"	"	10.30 AM - 4.30 PM	Squad drill, Musketry, Bayonet fighting & gas drill	
"	17 "	9 AM - 12 PM	Practice the lining up for the coming attack along the YPRES - COMINES railway and slow advance behind an improvised barrage	

Army Form C. 2118

WAR DIARY
or
INTELLIGENCE SUMMARY

(Erase heading not required.)

July/17
23 MX

Instructions regarding War Diaries and Intelligence Summaries are contained in F.S. Regs., Part II. and the Staff Manual respectively. Title pages will be prepared in manuscript.

Place	Date	Hour	Summary of Events and Information	Remarks and references to Appendices
THIEUSHOUK	17 July 17	4 PM - 7.30 PM	A Bombing use 15 Corps Range at R33	
		6 PM	Semi-final Divisional Football Competition Musketeers v R.A.M.C. Lost 1-0.	
		10 PM	Practice the lining up & slow advance behind barrage.	
"	18 July 17	2.30 PM	March to Corps training ground near BERTHEN.	
		6 PM	Zero hour for Brigade practice for the lining up and attack on YPRES - COMINES railway. Attack practiced	
		12 NOON	B & C Companies move to ReigiWood to be used for working parties for the R.E.s	
"	19 July	7.30 AM	Baths for Battalion at LA BESACE FARM.	
		2 PM - 4.30 PM	Battalion practice the lining up + slow advance behind barrage.	
"	20 July	9 AM - 12 NOON	Bayonet fighting. Musketry. Squad Drill.	
		2 PM - 4 PM	Preparation for the move of the 21st. 1 O.R. killed. 1 wounded.	
		10 PM	Practice lining up on Tapes. 11 A.M. reinforcements O.R. 2/Lt D.H Pickard joined battalion	
INFESTONTRSI "		9.30 AM	Left THIEUSHOUR and marched to CURRAGH CAMP near West Outre	
		1.30 PM	Battalion in CURRAGH CAMP. Encountered seek 2.O.R.	
~ "	22nd	9.30 AM	Church Parade	
		5 PM - 4.30 PM	Demonstration by Brigade Band outside Battalion HQrs.	

Army Form C. 2118.

WAR DIARY July 1/7
or
INTELLIGENCE SUMMARY.
(Erase heading not required.)

Instructions regarding War Diaries and Intelligence Summaries are contained in F. S. Regs., Part II. and the Staff Manual respectively. Title pages will be prepared in manuscript.

Place	Date	Hour	Summary of Events and Information	Remarks and references to Appendices
	23rd July 1917	4 A.M.	C.O. assumed in Command and Company Commanders journey to our Advanced new front-line and reconnoitre same.	23 MX
		3 P.M – 4 P.M	S.A.R.s exercises. Brigadier O.W.B. Gordon and Brigade Major J.F. Pragnall killed whilst returning from SPOIL BANK.	
		10 P.M.	Battalion practice the lining up on tapes for the attack. Capt J.L. Brown joined battalion & 2/Lt A.T. Taylor	
	24 July 1917.	3 P.M.	Battalion moved from CURRAGH CAMP and took over from the 15th Hants at UPPER MURUMBIDZEE CAMP (R64)	
		6 P.M.	Brigadier C.W.E. GORDON and Brigade Major J.F. Pragnall were buried at RENING HELST.	
		7 P.M.	B & C Companies rejoin Battalion from Ridge Wood. 5 O.R. wounded	
	25th July 1917	5.30 P.M.	Battalion move from UPPER MURUMBRIDGE CAMP by platoons at 50 yds interval and relieve the 21st London Regt in RIDGE WOOD.	
	26th July 1917.	9 A.M. – 12 NOON	Musketry instruction. All gas helmets and Box Respirators examined	
		6 P.M.	Working party for R.E. Found. Needles for carrying Evacuated sick 3 O.R.	
	27th July 1917		N.C.O. Runners and signals reconnoitre the front line and tracks areas	
		8 P.M.	Working party of 200 O.R. found for the R.E. 2 Killed 8 wounded O.R.s	
	28th July	2.30 A.M.	Ridge was shelled with gas shells. Evacuated sick 4 O.R	

Army Form C. 2118.

WAR DIARY July/17
or
INTELLIGENCE SUMMARY.
(Erase heading not required.)

(5)

23 MX

Place	Date	Hour	Summary of Events and Information	Remarks and references to Appendices
	July 30th/17	8.30 PM	The Battalion left Ridgewood for the trenches prior to attack. Encircled rech B.2.O.P. A Company via Oak Dumn O.4.25.8 Pontoon Bridge O.4.52.7 and O.0.f Avenue O.5.10.8 to New Trench at Frangeslan Spoil Bank O.5.01.5. B Company same route to Tunnel O.4.53.2 near Iron Bridge O.4b.2.4 2/Lt H.A. Gumm C Company to O.G.1 D Company via Blighty Bridge to O.G.2 There were no casualties up to this time. About 2 A.M. A and D Companies left their position for assembly area immediately in front of BATTLE WOOD. About 2 C Company replaced D Coy in O G 2. Forward area was being shelled with increasing severity as Companies approached assembly position as also BUFFS BANK and canal forward of Iron BRIDGE. The assembly of A & D Companies was just completed at Zero Hour IF 3.50 A.M. A Company formed the first two waves D Company formed the 2nd two waves. Two Vickers Guns and Teams assembled with A Coy. The remaining guns were moving	Mah. Sheet 28 S.W. Encircled rech B.2.O.P. 2/Lt H.A. Gumm " D.J. Hamilton } joined Battalion
	July 31st/17	3.50 AM	Barrage opens on German Front line and attack commenced. The ground between canal and Railway Embankment was found to be impassable owing to the wide expanse of water	

WAR DIARY
INTELLIGENCE SUMMARY

Army Form C. 2118

23 Mx

July 1/17

(6)

Place	Date	Hour	Summary of Events and Information	Remarks and references to Appendices
	July 31st		this compelled the majority of the troops to make their advance along the Railway Embankment itself. Red line was taken according to time table 3.54 P.M. but owing to the badstate of ground and the darkness, the barrage was moving too fast for the troops to keep close under it. After having the Red line waves 1, 3 & 4 came under Machine gun fire from dugouts on the Railway Embankment & the crest of the hill 50 yds from the left flank. Lieut Sutherland was killed and numerous casualties occurred at this juncture. Lieut Shribert was killed on the Railway Embankment by a bomb thrown from one of these occupied dug outs. Most of the wire had been cut but sufficient remained around water-logged shell holes near the Embankment to impede troops. Also from the Red to the Blue lines an exchange of ground varying in width from 10 to 35 yards was under water which made it impossible to rush the occupied dug outs from all sides. At zero + 45 minutes situation was as follows :- Lieuts Sherwood, Burney and Goulding and 40 other ranks & 3 Lewis Guns digging in on the Blue line at F.0.b.c. 9.50 - 9.50 in touch with America on the left but not in touch with 1.2.2 Brigade South of Canal. Lieut Humphrey and 20 other ranks digging in on Red line at O.5.a.6.5 in	

Army Form C. 2118.

WAR DIARY
or
INTELLIGENCE SUMMARY.

(Erase heading not required.)

July/17

23 MX

(7)

Place	Date	Hour	Summary of Events and Information	Remarks and references to Appendices
			in touch with Queens on left. Two dug outs at O.b.a. 50.30 with inmates were bung attacked by our men from the southern side of the Railway Embankment assisted by two Vickers Guns. At the time a bombing party now formerly Pte Thornycroft and 2/Lt Taylor who dropped down the Railway Embankment and approached the entrance dug outs from South West throwing bombs through the windows compelling the Germans to surrender. Eventually 40 prisoners were taken from the dug outs and sent back under escort a further was retained for stretcher bearing Forward Dress Quarters established in one of the dug outs at 5.40 A.M.	
July 31st 1917		6 A.M.	Blue Line had been reconnoitred and had been patrolled to the Canal Bank and former scheme of the enemy and one Lewis gun post put out at O b c 9.50 - 8.0. Lieut Trevor in charge with Mr Goulding & Mr Henry and 60 other ranks and 3 Lewis Guns. Mr Humphreys in Red Line with 20 other ranks. Machine Gun Officer with Vickers Gun with O.E. Enterprise in Railway Embankment dug out at O.b.a.6.4. One Trench Mortar with only 8 rounds of ammunition with O.E. Enterprise. Visual communication established with Battalion Head Quarters. All these positions were now under heavy M. Gun Fire from the dug outs still occupied at	

Army Form C. 2118.

WAR DIARY
or
INTELLIGENCE SUMMARY.

(Erase heading not required.)

July 1/17

23 MX

(8)

Instructions regarding War Diaries and Intelligence Summaries are contained in F. S. Regs., Part II. and the Staff Manual respectively. Title pages will be prepared in manuscript.

Place	Date	Hour	Summary of Events and Information	Remarks and references to Appendices
			at O b 6.3.5" and no movement could take place between them except by run ways. The positions were also located by enemy aeroplanes flying low down over the lines and shelled intermittently throughout the day. About 9 A.M. 2 Sergeants of the 11th Lumo arrived at Forward HQ giving names reporting that there were one officer and 14 other ranks of their Regt lying in 4 shell holes within 20 yards of these machine gun dug outs on the left flank. A and D companies remained in these positions throughout day and night of 31st and day time of 1st Aug. When they were relieved by B Coy owing to rain which commenced to fall heavily on the afternoon of the 31st July dug in chis on both Red and Blue line became knee deep in water, the garrison of the Red Line was placed in dug-outs in the Railway Embankment. 2/Lt G L Sutherland, J H Cleverence, & N Crothers killed 2/Lt F M Inwood wounded 14 O.Rs killed 121 O.Rs wounded 4 O.Rs missing.	

Major
Commanding 23rd Middlesex Regt.

23rd Middlesex Regt.

Army Form C. 2118.

WAR DIARY
or
INTELLIGENCE SUMMARY. August 1917

(Erase heading not required.)

Vol # 16

Place	Date	Hour	Summary of Events and Information	Remarks and references to Appendices
	August 1st		The positions were on the night of 30th/31st July were held by A and D Companies. B before was relieved the Battn with Tp throughout the day but quieted down at night.	
	" 2	P.M.	B Company relieved A in front line, A and D Companies carrying on Battn work. 2 O.R.s wounded 2 O.R.s missing.	
	August 3rd		Day fairly quiet.	
	" 3	7.30 P.M.	C Co. relieved D Co. in front line, B Co. carrying fatigues, nothing of further interest in O.G.2. B with Bttn on relief were very heavily bombed. Casualties 1 Officer 15 O.R.s killed 2nd Lieut .... 1 Officer & 7 O.R. wounded.	
	" 3	9 P.M.	Front line relieved. Bttn lightly shelled through the night.	
	"	9.30 P.M. – midnight	14th & Queens relieved the Battalion in the front line reserve positions	
	" 4th	3 A.M.	Battalion arrived at tunnels in SPOILBANK to rest before moving back ELZENWALLE CHATEAU. Casualties 5 O.R.	
		11 A.M.	moved by half Batttns to ELZENWALLE CHATEAU	
		3 P.M.	In search of "ELZENWALLE CHATEAU" A.D. 1 Officer wounded O.T.P.R. 2 O.R. struck off strength	
	" 5th		Day spent in cleaning up, making up necessary deficiencies, resting. Companies .... 3 O.R.s struck off strength	
	" 6th		Day spent in resting. 4 O.R.s attached to Pioneer Batt.	
	7th	7 P.M.	Battalion commenced to move up to the line, la Clytte from Reserve by infiltration	

WAR DIARY
or
INTELLIGENCE SUMMARY.
(Erase heading not required.)

Army Form C. 2118.

Place	Date	Hour	Summary of Events and Information	Remarks and references to Appendices
	Aug 7th	11 PM	B Company takes on position on front line. C Company in trenches on outside of YPRES – COMINES railway on left of BATTLE WOOD. D Company in supporting trench on centre of BATTLE WOOD. H Company and one section of M.G. Queens in Trenches on Canal Embankment at T.10.d.64.3	
	Aug 8th	2.30 AM	Relief of line reported complete. Day passed quietly. Wounded 1 OR. 1 Officer to England sick. 1 Officer to hospital sick.	
		6 PM	C Company relieves B in front line. C Company relieved in support on outside of Railway embankment. Wounded 2 OR	
	9th		Day passed quietly nothing of note happening. Wounded 4 OR. 4 OR sick to hospital	
	10th	3.45 AM	Enemy sprang mine out at O.8.c.3.5 casualties 19 Prisoners captured	
			28 R. Fusiliers	
	10th	11 PM	Company relieving battalion. Killed 1 OR wounded 3 OR. 1 Officer to England sick. 10 OR sick to hospital	
	11th	1.35 AM	Relief complete. WALLE	
		2 PM	Battalion proceeded by half platoons to ELZEN K CHATEAU remainder of platoon in skirmishing order resting. 1 Officer rejoins	
	12th	9 AM	Battalion march to METEREN by road.	
			Report on training of winter economy 1 Officer sick. Officer taken on strength Drafted 153 ORs in melanography ??? for inclusion by Coy Commander	

Army Form C. 2118

WAR DIARY
or
INTELLIGENCE SUMMARY.
(Erase heading not required.)

Instructions regarding War Diaries and Intelligence Summaries are contained in F. S. Regs., Part II. and the Staff Manual respectively. Title pages will be prepared in manuscript.

Place	Date	Hour	Summary of Events and Information	Remarks and references to Appendices
METEREN	Aug 15th		Inspection by Corps Commander.	
	16th		Coy instruction in preparing trenches. Draft of 20 arrived	
	17th		Squad drill, a short route march, and preparing for Army Commanders inspection	
	18th		Army Commanders inspection	
	19th	10.30 AM	Church parade. 2 Officers taken on strength 1 Rejoined	
	20th	11.30 AM	Left METEREN & marched to STAPLES	
STAPLES	21st	1.30 PM	Arrived in STAPLES.	
	22nd	9 AM	Leave STAPLES and marched to SETQUES	
SETQUES		5 PM	Arrived SETQUES	
	22nd		Feet inspection & bathing, remainder of day spent in resting. 2 Officers taken on strength	
	23rd — 27th	6	Squad drill. Musketry, bayonet fighting & Physical Training	
		3 PM		
	28th		B and D Coys being trained on range. B & C exchanging. B & D Coys carrying out firstaid Training. Everafternoon spent in	
			Bomb & trench mortar range. A & D exchanging. B & D Coy carrying tug of war games & signalling training under their respective Officers	

Army Form C. 2118.

WAR DIARY
or
INTELLIGENCE SUMMARY.
(Erase heading not required.)

Instructions regarding War Diaries and Intelligence Summaries are contained in F. S. Regs., Part II. and the Staff Manual respectively. Title pages will be prepared in manuscript.

Place	Date	Hour	Summary of Events and Information	Remarks and references to Appendices
SETQUES.	26th	6.30	Church parade	
	27th	9 AM–3 PM	Companies on Battalion training area. Reinforcements inspected by Divisional Gas Officer + Brigadier, inspected by O.C. 21st Divisional Train	
		3 PM	Demonstration of attack formation at X for School C.O. + Company Commanders. Strength 3 Officers taken on strength	
	28th	9 AM	Companies on Battalion training area. Mobility, Football, Baseball, Bayonet fighting. Returned H.H. Davis, draft	
		5 PM	and Physical Drill of 13 aur.	
	29th	9 AM	Companies on Battalion training area as on 28th	
		3 PM		
	30th	9 AM	Same as on 28th	
		3 PM		
	31st	9 AM–12 noon	Baths	
		1.30–3.30	March by new extended order drill	
			Horses reinoculated by the 2nd 2 M.O.'s 19 CM	
			and 12 M.M	

Signed
Lieut. Col.
O.C. 23rd Middlesex Regt.

WAR DIARY or INTELLIGENCE SUMMARY

Army Form C. 2118

23rd Reserve Regt

for September 1917

Place	Date	Hour	Summary of Events and Information	Remarks and references to Appendices
1917				
September	1	9am to 12noon	Religious - Kit inspection, Berlice & Bayonet training. 3 OR struck off strength	Oct 17
	2	10am	Church parade with R.W. Kents. - 3 OR struck off strength 13 OR taken on	
	3		Route practice method of attack, Musketry & Physical, 1 OR struck off strength	
	4		Training in training area	
	5			
	6		Demonstration Aeroplane contact. Battalion sports. 20 OR struck off strength	
	7		Brigade sports. 20 OR struck off strength. 1 Officer struck off strength, 3 Officers taken on strength	
	8		Divisional field days. Practising method of attack. 30 OR struck off strength. 29 OR taken on	
	9		Range at V.2.d.5.4. moved by Battn. transport. Left for Ridge Wood 20 OR struck off	
	10	2pm 5pm	Battalion left by buses for Ridge Wood. 3 OR struck off. 4 OR taken on. 1 Officer taken on strength	1 OR killed 8 wounded
	18		Arrives Ridge Wood, took over shelters and tents	say to Belenhoff Camp
			Working parties for 41st Div. Signals and 228 & 239 Field	5 taken on strength
			R.E. Engineers. Parties prepared shelter trenches at Cane Wood	12 Sept 1 Officer wounded
	19	9am	Packing Kits. Details left for detail camp.	17" 1 "
		1pm	All work ceased.	" "
		8.30pm	Battn. proceeded to Zack Wood and took up position in trenches	
			Quiet night. Very little shelling.	

WAR DIARY or INTELLIGENCE SUMMARY

23rd Middlesex Regt. Army Form C. 2118.

Place	Date	Hour	Summary of Events and Information	Remarks and references to Appendices
1914				
Sept	20	5:10am	Barrage opened at 5.10am. Advance commenced. 17th Brigade on right. 13th Brigade on left. Left Brigade advanced to first objection but owing to lack of support had to fall back on to Blue Line. Right Brigade checked beyond Red Line.	
		10:30am	Barrage ceased.	
		1pm	123 Brigade ordered to reinforce firing line and take second objective. DLI on left. RWK on centre. Middlesex on Right.	
		2pm	Battn arrived at Canada Tunnels.	
		4:30pm	Advance towards firing line was known as Lac in Artillery formation, toward machine gun fire from front and right flank.	
		5:30pm	Arrive at Java Trench, encounter	
		6:30pm	New barrage opened on ridge and dugouts in front, strongly held by snipers and machine guns. Bn. & Coys advancing in extended formation by short rushes to Blue Line, but owing to heavy fire were unable to hold its strength. The ground was very soft and cut up by shell fire, this and the amount of ammn.	

WAR DIARY or INTELLIGENCE SUMMARY

Army Form C. 2118.

23rd Middlesex Regt.

Place	Date	Hour	Summary of Events and Information	Remarks and references to Appendices
1917 September	20		encountered made further progress impracticable. The Bradford Line assumed a very close nature, until the tiny nets on the immediate front were cleared. There we held on an advanced line, the remainder of the Battalion consolidating in depth, the rear company being on the eastern bank of the Ravinsville Beck, with orders to hold all positions until daybreak. Enemy concentrated on ridge on front, dispersed by Lewis Gun and rifle fire. ORs 10 killed 71 wounded 21 missing 3 gassed death 1 Officer wounded.	
		8pm		
		10pm	Patrols sent as far as Blue Line, reported all clear. Shelling & sniping continued all night.	
	21	5am	Scouts despatched to ascertain exact position of troops on our left flank.	
		5:30am	"B" Coy sent on to ridge on left flank with orders to attack an enemy flank in conjunction with our frontal attack.	
		9:30am	"C" & "A" Coys advanced in short rushes taking cover	

WAR DIARY
or
INTELLIGENCE SUMMARY

Army Form C. 2118.

23rd Middlesex Regt.
for October 1917

Place	Date	Hour	Summary of Events and Information	Remarks and references to Appendices
1917				
Septen	21	9.30am	on shell holes until the open on the Passchendaele were reached, hostile machine gun fire was very intense and casualties numerous, the ground from here forward was found to be practically a quagmire and further advance was impossible without entailing enormous casualties, an advanced line was then pushed forward and the Battalion dug in. 1 Officer killed 3 wounded.	
		4pm	Enemy attempted to counterattack but were held in check by Lewis gun & rifle fire and the barrage opened up and annihilated them. O.R.s 4 killed 47 wounded & Missing 64 from which 11Th portions shelled by 5.9. Enemy snipers kept in check 1 Officer killed	
	22		by rifle fire.	
	23	3am	Hertos arrive to relieve Battn.	
	24	5am	Lost company relieved, the Battalion then proceeded to Micmac Camp, on arrival received orders to link up with details and B Coy at Hondeghem, 2d ORs joined Battn	

WAR DIARY
or
INTELLIGENCE SUMMARY.

(Erase heading not required.)

Army Form C. 2118.

23rd Middlesex Regt. 1 Septr 1917

Place	Date	Hour	Summary of Events and Information	Remarks and references to Appendices
1917				
Septem	25	9am	Rifle and feet inspections. Remainder of day – Rest. Transport left for Londrekerque.	
	26	7am	Buses at Honeyham arrived Wargger Brigge 11.30 am, marched to billets at Londrekerque.	
	27	6am	Left Londrekerque marching	
		9.30am	Arrived at Bray Dunes and took over position from 2/8 Z.3. Remainder of day. Bathing & rest 2 smash off tonight	
	28	9am	Inspections – Rifle, feet & gas helmets.	
		1pm	Bathing.	
	29	9am	Gas demonstration for Battalion. 2smash off tonight.	
		1pm	Bathing Parade	
	30	9.30am	Church Parade.	

[signature]
Lt Colonel
Commanding 23rd Middlesex Regt
1/10/17

23rd Bn. Middlesex Regt.

WAR DIARY for Month of October 1917

INTELLIGENCE SUMMARY

Army Form C. 2118.

Vol 18

Place	Date	Hour	Summary of Events and Information	Remarks and references to Appendices
BRAY-DUNES	1/10/17		Battalion in training. Two Coffs. Musky G, PT & BF in morning. Sports and Inter Coy Games	
	2/10/17		Day spent in training	
	3/10/17		Ditto	
	4/10/17		Company use Rifle Range	
ST. IDESBALD	5/10/17	11.30 AM	Battalion relieved by 2nd Grenadier Guards & move to ST. IDESBALD B.6.6.5 near N.E. Suburban Travelling Coy	
MIDDLEKERKE CAMP R27 C.3.3	6/10/17	9.30 AM 11.30 PM	Company relieves 18 Royal Fusiliers near seawall. Go. Coys move to Middlekerke Camp at R27 C.3.3 & relieves 1/5th Manchesters in support Battalion assumes a very careful command. Relief of Royal troops of Battalion Coys not in training	
	7/10/17		Full scale Sandbagging of huts. Relief 2 officers & NCOs reconnoitre front line	
	8/10/17		Work of huts continued with Party of 5 officers & NCOs reconnoitre front line	
	9/10/17		Battn at OOST DUNKIRKE allotted to latrine X30.9.3 the 4th Bn relieve of 3rd Bn Relief of Officer while accompaniment front line	
	10/10/17		Day spent in training. 3 officers & 14 NCOs reconnoitre front line	
	11/10/17		Day spent in training	

WAR DIARY
or
INTELLIGENCE SUMMARY.

(Erase heading not required.)

23rd Middlesex Regt. Army Form C. 2118.

Place	Date	Hour	Summary of Events and Information	Remarks and references to Appendices
Oost Dunkerke Bains	11/10/17	6pm	Battalion (350 strong) leave Middlesex Camp for front line. "B" Coy with Australian Tunnelling Co. remainder of Battn. left at Middlesex Camp to proceed with tramway.	
Nieuport Bains	12/10/17	12mn	Relief of 30 D.L.I. completed, on left one section of left division Battn. H.Q. in M.19.a.2.9. "B" Coy on right, "C" Coy on left and "A" Coy in support, during the night trench mortars were very active against our right Coy, otherwise quiet. Patrols sent out, found no trace of the enemy. Enemy artillery active, heavy trench mortars and Minenwerfer were used against our trenches but silenced by our artillery. Battn. H.Q. and back areas shelled by 5.9" hows.	
	13/10/17		Our patrols very active on canal, our patrol across the canal reconnoitred 200 yds of enemies ground, the enemy discovered it & Minnies used by enemy against our front line. Back areas shelled with 5.9 & 4.2. Retaliation by our artillery. Otherwise very quiet on front. Patrols out all night.	

WAR DIARY or INTELLIGENCE SUMMARY

Army Form C. 2118.

33rd Middlesex Regt.

Instructions regarding War Diaries and Intelligence Summaries are contained in F.S. Regs., Part II. and the Staff Manual respectively. Title pages will be prepared in manuscript.

(Erase heading not required.)

Place	Date	Hour	Summary of Events and Information	Remarks and references to Appendices
Nieuport Bains	14/10/17		Front quiet, usual shelling from TMs & heavy artillery. Patrols out on both Coy fronts. Lewis Coy sent out warning party.	
	15/10/17		Front very quiet.	
		3pm	Relief by 26 R.F. begins (L.Guns only)	
		6pm	26 R.F. Lewises begin relief.	
		9.30pm	Relief completed. Battalion moves off to camp at La Panne.	
			Non 7th entrained between Duttons.	
La Panne	16/10/17	12.30am	Last company arrives at camp W.22.B.55 Officers billeted in La Panne. B Company remain with Australian Tunnellers.	
			Remainder of day spent on checking deficiencies	
	17/10/17	9am	Training under company arrangements	
	18/10/17	4.30pm		
	19/10/17		Company and specialist training. A & B Coy on range W.19.a	
	20/10/17	9.30am	Battalion Parade	
		10.30	"A Coy" Route march	
		1pm	C & B Specialists carry on training	
	21/10/17		Church Parade (C of E, Non conformist & R.C.)	

A6945 Wt. W1442/M160 350,000 12/16 D.D. & L. Forms/C/2118/14

WAR DIARY or INTELLIGENCE SUMMARY.
(Erase heading not required.)

Army Form C. 2118. 23rd Middlesex Regt.

Place	Date	Hour	Summary of Events and Information	Remarks and references to Appendices
La Panne	October 1917 20		"G" Coy allotted baths at St Idesbalde	
	21	9am	Minor tactical scheme. Bad shots on miniature range.	
		2.30pm	Build & bayonet training. Specialist schools continue training	
	22		Wet day, all training programmes cancelled.	
	23	11.30am	Lecture by Major Gayer on camp. All companies & schools carry on training.	
		1am 11.45pm 2 & 3.45am	Demonstration of attack on dug outs. PT and drill.	
	24	11.30am	Inspection of camp and training by Divisional General.	
			Inspection of "A" Coy by CO. "B" Coy & HQ Co. inspected by OC	
			"C" Coy proceed to canal at E.2.d.4.2. to practice forming	
		1.30pm	"D" Coy. "A" & HQ Cos proceed to canal to practice forming	
			First practice at 3pm second at 4pm. Teas at canal	
	25		Sandbagging of all huts proceeded with. No training of companies or schools except returned engineers.	
	26	10.30am	Inspection of "G" & "B" Coy by CO	

WAR DIARY 23rd Middlesex Regt. Army Form C.

WAR DIARY or INTELLIGENCE SUMMARY.
(Erase heading not required.)

Place	Date	Hour	Summary of Events and Information	Remarks and references to Appendices
La Panne	1914 October 27		Company training (Morning miniature range by Gun etc)	
	28		Inspection of Battn. Hd Qrs. by Adjutant	
			Church parade for both non-conformists R.C's	
	29	9am	"D" Coy field practices on range	
			Warning orders received by Battalion	
			Remainder of day "Battalion" checking & issuing advances kit underclothes	
			"B" Coy report Battalion	
		7.55pm	Air raid, one bomb dropped on camp, 1 killed, 4 wounded	
		10.9am	Battalion route march (Furnes Adinkerke La Panne)	
		12 noon	Wet day. Battalion returns to camp	
		3pm	Inspection of feet	
		4pm	"A" & "B" Coys Route march. "C" & "D" Coys Company training	
	31	9am		
		11am	Rect. & Cert. inspection by all companies	
		12.15pm	Lecture by C.O. on "Protection" — Advance guards	
		2.30pm	Company training	
			Other Officers carry out "Advance Guard" practice	

Lieut. Colonel
Commanding 23rd Middlesex
B Coy Commanding 23rd Middlesex Regt.

www.ingramcontent.com/pod-product-compliance
Lightning Source LLC
Chambersburg PA
CBHW081550160426
43191CB00011B/1886